Double Luck

Memoirs

OF A

Chinese Orphan

1964

Double Luck

Memoirs

OF A

Chinese Orphan

BY

Lu Chi Fa

WITH

Becky White

Holiday House

NEW YORK

Acknowledgements

I wish to acknowledge, with a double portion of gratitude,
Chi Fa and Karen Grencik. I humbly bow to Chi Fa,
the Chinese orphan whose story is told herein.
I also wish to thank Karen for her unwavering
confidence in my abilities.
B.W.

The authors would like to thank Professor Gary Steenson,
California Polytechnic University,
and Roy for researching and providing the family tree.

10 11 12
Library of Congress Cataloging-in-Publication Data

Lu, Chi Fa.
Double luck : memoirs of a Chinese orphan / by Lu Chi Fa with Becky White.
p.   cm.
Summary: Tells the story of the author's struggles after being
orphaned at the age of three and how he held on to his dream
of coming to the United States as he passed from one relative
to another and was even sold to a Communist couple.
ISBN 0-8234-1560-0 (hardcover)
1. Lu, Chi Fa—Childhood and youth—Juvenile literature.   2. Chinese
Americans— Biography—Juvenile literature.   3. Orphans—China—
Biography—Juvenile literature.   4. Children—Communist
countries—Biography—Juvenile literature.   5. China—Biography—
Juvenile literature.   [1. Lu, Chi Fa—Childhood and youth.   2. Orphans.
3. China—Social life and customs—1949–1976.]   I. White, Becky.   II. Title.
E184.C5 L75 2001
304.8'73051'092—dc21
[B]   99-048509

ISBN-13: 978-0-8234-1560-1

For Sister

L. C. F.

1959

Contents

Double Luck

Memoirs
OF A
Chinese
Orphan

1962

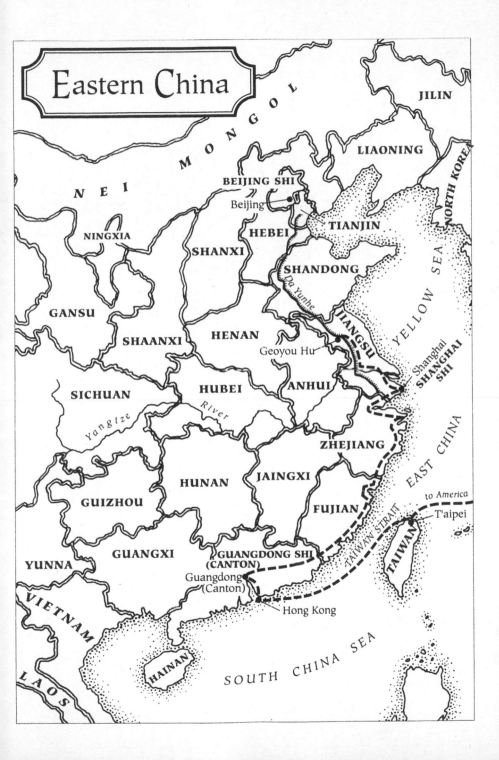

Eastern China

JILIN

NEI MONGOL

LIAONING

NINGXIA

BEIJING SHI

Beijing

HEBEI

TIANJIN

SHANXI

SHANDONG

NORTH KOREA

GANSU

SHAANXI

HENAN

Da Yunhe

JIANGSU

YELLOW SEA

Geoyou Hu

Shanghai

SHANGHAI SHI

SICHUAN

HUBEI

ANHUI

Yangtze

River

ZHEJIANG

EAST CHINA

HUNAN

JAINGXI

to America

GUIZHOU

FUJIAN

T'aipei

YUNNA

GUANGXI

GUANGDONG SHI
(CANTON)

Guangdong
(Canton)

TAIWAN

TAIWAN STRAIT

VIETNAM

Hong Kong

LAOS

HAINAN

SOUTH CHINA SEA

PART I

JIANGSU PROVINCE

1944–1950

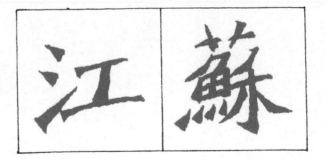

Lu Chi Fa and his nephew c. 1949

1
Sister's House

(Be Strong)

堅 強

We slept, three, in the big straw bed, Papa, Mama, and me. One night, summer's only storm split the sky with a sharp, crackling light, and I heard Mama scream, *"Nooooooo!"*

Thunder shook our little house. "Wake up," I begged Papa. "Wake up."

But Papa didn't wake up. Papa was dead. It is very sad to say, but my first recollection of being part of a family was the night my father died. I was only three years old.

Sister said that at the funeral Mama knelt on one side of the bed and I stood on the other side, clutching the quilt that draped him. We were two broken hearts that sobbed as one.

Father died in the summer of 1944, the year of the monkey. Memories of Mama and Papa are secondhand stories told to me by my only sister, Shiow Jen. Sister said Father had had a heat stroke. The village healer came to our house, and after looking at Father, he handed my mother a small rice-paper package of powder. "Sprinkle this in his tea," he instructed.

After Papa swallowed the tea, he went to sleep. It wasn't until the angry storm awoke her in the middle of the night that Mama realized Papa was resting in an eternal sleep.

After the funeral, the healer told Mama, "The wrong medicine—unfortunate accident. I am sorry."

"Unfortunate accident!" cried Mama. "Sorry?"

Mama left the man standing in our living room and went straight to her bedroom and crawled into bed, never to get out again. So Father's passing was only half of a double pain I had to endure—a pain that lives within me still. A few days after Papa's funeral, brokenhearted, Mama followed him into the hereafter.

All together my parents left a family of five children. I, Lu Chi Fa, was the baby. My three brothers and one sister were much older than I—grown-ups before I was born.

My father was a traditional businessman who owned an old-fashioned wood-and-brick department store. Papa had inherited the store from his father, who had inherited it from his father, and so on back many generations for more than one hundred years. In our little village, Mao Cho Wei, Father's store was the place where elders met to talk and women bought shirts, perfume, silk cloth, and groceries.

My mother, like most Chinese women, kept house and took care of the children. She was an artist who did beautiful needlework. When I think of Mama, I picture a fair face, glowing like a full moon. Sister said I was the joy of my papa, his favorite son, son of his old age. I was loved by a beautiful mother and was part of a good and loving family. But the bad fortune of two untimely deaths left me an orphan, a small boy in a world where no one wanted me. The only thing I had that my parents gave to me was my name, Chi Fa, which means "new beginning."

Sister was named Shiow Jen, which means "pretty treasure." She was both pretty and a treasure. She had a good heart. Over the years, many times Sister rescued me from misfortune. Before my parents died, one of Mama's sisters had arranged for Sister to marry Fan Chi Haw, a deaf man. He was rich and lived in a big house. In the middle of his house was a courtyard with a brick well where he could draw his own water. In those days, only the wealthiest people had their own well inside their house. In the first months after my parents died, I lived in the big house with Sister and Chi Haw. I don't remember many things about Sister's husband except that he had very big ears. I wondered, *With such big ears, why is it that Chi Haw cannot hear?*

Sister said that I forgot the words I had learned to speak before my parents died, and I did not try to learn new ones. Day after day I sat on the ground of the courtyard, near the well, in a world of silence. One thing I remember clearly is finding a cricket. Sister put it in a little wooden box, and I carried it around with me. At night I took out my cricket and listened to its songs.

One autumn night, when big black clouds hid the full moon's light, I was lying in my bed, about to fall asleep. I heard Sister weeping softly. There were no words, just muffled sobs. My heart knew that the problem was Chi Fa.

The next morning the look on her face told me that Sister was very sad. Chi Haw sat at the table slurping his tea and rice porridge. I tried to be silent as I ate my breakfast. I thought that if I didn't look at them, they might forget I was there. I swallowed the porridge and slipped from the kitchen without making a sound.

Soon I heard Chi Haw leaving the house. I listened to the clinking of Sister washing the dishes in the kitchen. Then she came and drew water from the well. I watched her pour it into a big wooden tub. To take the chill off the water, she added a pot of boiling water from the stove. "Come to Sister," she told me.

Lowering my eyes, I obeyed.

She undressed me and put me in the warm water. While she scrubbed me and washed my hair, she sang.

Row, row, row to sea.
Grandma's on the bridge.
Grandma calls to me,
"What a good baby."

When Sister finished her song, I heard sniffling sounds. She took me to the kitchen and stood me in front of the warm stove, where she dried and dressed me. She combed and braided my hair. She handed me the box with my cricket inside and said, "Chi Fa, you are a very good and quiet little boy. Sister likes to have you here, but Chi Haw does not. I am going to have a baby, and my husband wants only his own son. There is nothing I can do."

I was only three and a half years old, and although I hadn't spoken since my parents' death, I understood everything I heard. I felt the pain of Sister's words. A sob pushed out of me like a giant bird escaping from a very small cage. Sister took me by the hand and led me to the road. "Come along," she said.

Using hurried steps, Sister glided over the dusty road. Following on her heels, I heard her say over and over, "Chi Fa must be strong." Once she stopped and squatted and put her face near mine. Holding my chin in her hand, she said, "Promise me you will never forget that you are a good boy."

I nodded.

When we got to Uncle's house, I looked into Sister's tearstained face and pleaded with my eyes, but she turned and knocked on the door. Before walking away, Sister said something I would never forget. "Chi Fa, you are lucky. Good fortune will find you." Then she left me standing alone at the door.

If Chi Fa is lucky, I asked myself, *why is Sister giving me away?*

When the door swung open, Aunt was wearing her crankiest face. Favorite Uncle's wife did not know Sister was bringing me to live with them. She opened her beady eyes as wide as she could and stared down the road where Sister had kicked up the dust in her hurry to escape. "Shiow Jen, come back here! Take this brother of yours! We do not want another mouth to feed!" shouted Aunt.

Then Aunt grunted and went back inside and slammed the door shut. I stood on the stoop and waited. I thought Aunt would come back and open the door for me, or maybe Sister would reappear. I waited and I waited. I wanted to run away, but I had nowhere to go.

I stood at the door all that gray day, listening to the sounds inside. When morning slipped silently into afternoon, I wondered if my cricket was as hungry as I was. So I found a small leaf and put it inside the cricket's cage. Then I sat down on the stoop and listened as my cricket sang Sister's words: "Be strong. Be strong."

It was a relief to me when finally I saw Favorite Uncle coming up the dirt road. He was a teacher who taught in our village's only grade school. Favorite Uncle was a small, handsome man. "What are you doing standing here, youngster?" he asked, patting my head. "Come inside."

In those first few days at Uncle's house, I could not have felt worse. Aunt never looked at me. She pretended I was not there, which was just as well because I was afraid of her. Aunt was a round, pudgy woman, much taller and wider than Uncle. She did not have bound feet like traditional Chinese women whose feet had been wrapped tightly in strips of linen to keep them from growing. I clearly remember looking at her feet and thinking how huge they were. From where I stood, my eyes only a few feet off the ground, when I looked up past her belly into her flaring nostrils, Aunt looked like a wild boar.

Every day Aunt stomped around the two rooms, huffing giant sighs that got louder as the days grew darker. In the afternoons, when Uncle would come home from school, he would bundle us up and take my cousins and me for a walk up the dirt road, all the way to the river. Uncle's son, who was three years older than I, would run along the bank and throw rocks into the water. But his daughter and I would sit quietly on either side of him and listen to his ghost stories. In his tales, Uncle described brave boys and girls who gallantly stood up to ghosts. They would yell, "Go away, Ghost! We are not afraid of you!"

I liked Uncle's stories about courageous children. Uncle's daughter was the same age as I. Often he would tease us and say when we grew up we would be married to each other. That made us giggle. It was peaceful on the riverbank, watching clouds play hide-and-seek with the sun. Even the stench of fish being cleaned by nearby fishermen was perfume to me. Favorite Uncle made me feel safe. I would have liked to have crawled under his shirt and stayed there forever. I wanted to be his boy.

One day, as we watched the water flowing by, Uncle said, "The river grows deeper and wider as it flows home to the sea. Like you, Chi Fa. You will grow deeper and wider as you go, and someday you will be home."

Only a curtain divided the kitchen from the room where Uncle and Aunt slept. My cousins and I slept on mats on the kitchen floor. One spring night, when a full moon rose high and lit the house as bright as day, Aunt was especially cranky. I could hear Uncle trying to soothe her as she stomped about like a rooting boar. Poor Uncle.

"The boy is four, and he cannot even talk," she huffed. "What good is he? He's just another mouth to feed."

"He is my sister's baby," Uncle pleaded softly.

"Give him back to Shiow Jen. Why should we be responsible for him?" Aunt demanded.

"Shiow Jen has a new baby girl to take care of, and Chi Haw doesn't want him," Uncle whispered.

"I don't want him either!" she snapped. "Tomorrow he goes."

Then came silence. Aunt always got the last word.

The next morning, by the time I awoke, Uncle had already gone to school. Aunt gave me a little bowl of rice porridge, and then without the bath that Sister had given me on my first moving day, she grabbed my hand and pulled me to the road. "Hurry along," she ordered as she stomped on. There were no words of encouragement from Aunt as she waddled up the road ahead of me.

I can talk! I wanted to shout. *I will talk to you, Aunt. I won't eat very much. Please let me stay with Favorite Uncle.* I had so many thoughts, but I did not speak. Like a lamb, I followed her up the hill. When we reached the house of another of my mother's brothers, Aunt knocked and left me standing at the door. Alone.

Over the next two years, I lived in many different houses. I learned to talk, but still no one wanted to take me in. I lived with this uncle and that uncle, with this brother and that brother, back and forth. When one family got tired of me, they passed me off to another relative. Each time I was sent away, I wept. To know that no one wants you is a terrible thing.

In the summer of 1946, the year of the dog, I was five and a half years old. Behind closed doors, it had been decided by Sister and uncles that since Number One Brother, Ching Fa, had inherited the family store, he should take care of me. So I went to live with my eldest brother, his wife, and their son, who was one year younger than I.

Ching Fa liked to play games of chance and drink rice wine. He liked to pretend he was wealthy, a big spender. But Ching Fa wasn't rich. He foolishly gambled away all the profits of the family store. He dishonored our ancestors and Father, all of whom had worked hard to make the store a successful business. Eventually Brother lost the store to gambling debts, and, shamed in our village, he ran away to a big city called Shanghai.

Sister-in-Law, Nephew, and I waited many days, but Ching Fa never returned. Shanghai was much too far for a woman and two little boys to travel by foot, and Sister-in-Law did not have the money for us to take the barge, so we waited and waited for Brother to come home. After several months, Sister-in-Law said she had bought barge tickets to Shanghai. I wondered where she could have gotten that much money. That same day, as the sun set and changed the blue sky to pink, we three set out on the road toward the canal.

I was glad to get to go to the big city, Shanghai, but I wished I could say goodbye to Sister. Did Sister know where I was going?

We walked until we reached the canal at twilight. Nearly hidden in a patch of bamboo were a man and a woman and their very small boat.

Leaving Nephew and me standing in the road, Sister-in-Law went up to the strangers and bowed. She turned and pointed to me. The man gave a small nod to Sister-in-Law and signaled with a motion of his hand for me to come closer. I was afraid, so I did not move. Then Sister-in-Law came and grabbed my hand. "Come," she commanded.

She pulled me over to the man and woman and then gave me a little shove.

Listening to their conversation, I learned where Sister-in-Law had gotten the money for the barge tickets. She had sold me to the man, a Communist chief, for five hundred pounds of rice, which she used to pay for her and Nephew to take the barge to Shanghai. While she talked to the strangers, she didn't let her eyes meet mine. Then, without turning back or waving good-bye, she went to Nephew and took his hand, and they hurried down the canal road.

As I stood on the bank between the two strangers, I did not know to be afraid. This was my thinking: *So much bad luck, maybe now good luck has found me.* I did not know that the misery I had endured so far was only a small measure of the pain waiting on the path ahead.

2
Riding on a Dragon
(Be Obedient)

順 從

As soon as the stranger touched me to lift me onto the boat, I knew that this was not a fortunate thing. I crouched in the boat and gazed up at the sky. The farther we drifted from my home village, the more afraid I became. Worried thoughts kept me awake. *Where are we going? Will I ever see Sister and Favorite Uncle again? Can I trust these strangers?*

After drifting most of the night, the moon rose—a silver sliver shaped like a little boat. We were twins, the moon sailing on the horizon and the little boat drifting along in the narrow canal. By the time the moon had sailed to the top of the sky, we had reached the man's house. Limp with misery, I pretended to be asleep. The man carried me into the house and put me to bed between him and his wife. I slept that whole day and the next night through. I didn't want to open my eyes or face another day in a new place.

I don't remember the name of the Communist chief who paid five hundred pounds of rice for me. He was middle-aged and had recently married for the first time. His new wife had a twenty-year-old son. Communist Father reasoned that his stepson was too old for him to train, but I was a very small boy, and in his eyes, I was still trainable. Little Chi Fa would make an obedient son. Communist Father said that his stepson was Number One Son and I was Number Two Son. We made him twice lucky. That was how I got my new name, Shang Shii, which means "double luck."

In the beginning, Communist Father and his wife seemed to like me. They asked me to call them Father and Mother. They gave me a pair of blue cotton pants, a blue shirt, and a pair of shoes made of straw. They said I was their baby. Sometimes they were nice to me, but other times they were very cruel. From day to day, I did not know what to expect. I quickly learned that I could not trust them. Soon they began to distance themselves from me, too. Instead of sleeping with them in the big straw bed, I was put on a mat, on the floor, in the kitchen. All around the house I could see the signs: this was another family that didn't want me.

In those days in China, there was little charcoal to use in the stoves. Instead, people used straw and bamboo that had been dried under the sun. I learned how to put the straw and bamboo into the stove, so that became my job. During the Celebration of the Moon, which is in August, the women make very small, sweet rice cakes. On the day of the celebration, I was in the kitchen stuffing the straw and bamboo into the stove while Communist Mother made the sweet rice cakes. She piled a big platter many, many high. Then she said, "Oh, Double Luck, please take these rice cakes and give them to the Buddha."

In many Chinese living rooms, there is a picture or sculpture of Buddha. It is a Chinese custom that before eating, some food is placed before Buddha to show respect. It is believed that this will bring the family peace and good luck.

In the Communist parents' house, Buddha's picture was quite high. I was just a little boy, so I had to climb to reach it. As I placed the first batch of cakes in front of the Buddha, I looked around to see if Communist Mother was watching. Not seeing her, I quickly put two or three sweet cakes into my pocket so that while I was putting the straw and bamboo into the stove I could enjoy the sweets. I did this several times. I don't know exactly how many cakes went from the platter to my pocket to my hungry mouth.

Later, when she realized some of the cakes were missing, Communist Mother said, "Oh, Double Luck, the stack of cakes for the Buddha was this high." She showed me how high with her hands. "Now it is only this high," she said, indicating with her hands again. "How many did you eat?"

I lowered my eyes and looked at my feet. "I don't know. Maybe two. Maybe three."

She grabbed me by my ear and twisted hard. I lost my balance and landed on the floor. Kicking me, she scolded, "You lie to me! You ate more than just two or three. You are a disgusting little thing! You are worse than disgusting." Then out of her twisted mouth came, "You are a liar and a thief!"

I am not a liar or a thief, I thought. I kept my promise to Sister, and in my mind I repeated, *I am a good boy.*

That night, when Communist Father came home, she told him the story of how I ate the Buddha's cakes. With each sentence Communist Father's face grew redder and redder. By the time she finished her exaggeration, he looked purple as a beet. He started yelling, "Double Luck, you are just a little baby, a little devil. You lie all the time."

I wasn't lying. I liked sweet rice cakes, and I was hungry because they didn't feed me enough. I was not a thief. Naturally a little boy will eat cakes if he gets the chance. But out of respect, I could not explain or talk back to Communist Father.

He yelled, "Tell me the truth!"

"I am telling the truth, Father," I sobbed with fear.

My hair had never been cut, and my pigtail hung down my back. In those days, when a Chinese boy had a pigtail, it meant he was a favored child of his parents. When Communist Father didn't like my answer, he yanked my pigtail. He grabbed me by my hair and hung me up in the air with my feet dangling several feet from the floor. The pain was excruciating. I screamed and screamed, but Communist Father wouldn't let me down.

Sister, I need you, I thought over and over. *Sister, come and save me.*

As hair ripped from my scalp, tears streamed down my face. Misery welled up inside me. *If ever I have a son,* I promised myself, *I will never bring him pain.*

After what seemed like a very long time, Communist Father dropped me to the floor. I hoped my punishment was over, but it was not. Next he grabbed me by my ankles and hung me upside down. His tight grip hurt. Wiggling to free myself only brought more pain. I screamed, "Please, someone, help me!" My voice sounded strange. It came not from my throat, but from somewhere deep inside me. It was a little voice I hardly recognized. Dangling upside down, I felt part of me slipping away, seeping out of me like the tears that puddled on the floor beneath my head. "Please, someone, help me," I begged some more. Soon I was too exhausted to make a sound. Silently I hung there as a nearby cricket sang, "Be strong. Be strong."

After some time, a neighbor came along, and he said, "Oh, you shouldn't. He's just a little boy. You are very cruel to be doing this."

Shamed by his neighbor, Communist Father dropped me to the floor.

Weak from the punishment, I crawled into the

kitchen and curled up in a tight little ball. Not knowing if the attack was over, I put my hands and arms
up over my head and fell unconscious.

That night, for the first time, I dreamed I was flying on the back of a dragon. It was a big, strong
dragon. I rode on the winged beast's back all night. I
felt safe and powerful in my dream. When I awoke,
my bruised body ached, but I soothed myself with
thoughts of my mighty dragon. I had been taught
that dreams were signs of things to come, so I wondered, *What could such a dream mean?*

Winter was especially cold that year. Each day
when the Communist parents went out, I was left
home alone, locked outside on the porch like a dog.
Most days, with nothing to eat, I waited many hours
for their return. I remember one day when black
clouds hung low enough to touch and icy sleet
soaked my clothes, I nearly froze. My straw shoes
could not keep out the wet and cold. I tried to be
brave, but in the end, I could not ignore my freezing
limbs and empty belly. Finally Communist Brother's
wife came. She said, "Oh, Double Luck, I feel so
sorry for you. They treat you so badly." Then she
said, "Let me fix you something to eat."

She took me inside, and what happened next is
something I recall clearly. She gave me a big spoon-
ful of pork fat. Cold and famished, I swallowed the
fat in one giant gulp. She wasn't being mean. She
was just simple and didn't know any better. She
thought that because I was thin, maybe a little fat in

my body would do me some good. But oh, afterward my stomach ached. It felt like a hungry dog was ripping at my belly. I was sick for many days.

Because I didn't get enough to eat, I thought about food most of the time. But I was sometimes distracted from the gnawing in my belly as I anticipated the pleasure of the coming New Year's celebration.

The Chinese New Year begins at sunset on the second new moon each winter. It is celebrated with sweets. Rice balls with black sesame seeds inside were my favorite. To a boy, these rice balls are like candy. It is a Chinese belief that eating a sweet rice ball means a person will have good luck all through the coming year. On the other hand, if a person doesn't eat the sweet cakes on New Year's, misfortune and bad luck are sure to find him. When I woke up New Year's morning 1947, the year of the pig, Communist Mother and Father were up and talking in the kitchen. She said, "Oh, Double Luck, you may sleep longer. Don't get up."

She had never said that to me before. At the time I thought, *She is saying that so I will miss the treats and attract bad luck to myself.*

I needed to get up to go to the toilet, but I tried to do as I was told and stay put on the floor. With my eyes tightly shut, I tried to go back to sleep. I stayed on the floor until my belly hurt. Then I could stand it no longer. I knew I might get my ear twisted or my head smacked, but I had to get up. As I rushed passed them to the toilet, I heard them laughing at me.

Hoping for a sweet rice ball, soup, or something, I hurried back into the kitchen. With nostrils flared as though she smelled something nasty, she asked, "Did you wash your hands?"

Giving her my best good-morning smile, I said, "Yes, Mother." I forced myself to be especially pleasant. I said, "Oh, Happy New Year, Mother. Happy New Year, Father." But I did not get a sweet rice ball with sesame seeds that New Year's morning. Instead, Communist Mother gave me a bowl of plain rice. She and Communist Father ate all the sweet treats. And sure enough, the coming year, misfortune and bad luck found me.

The Communist parents continued chastising me in many different ways. Sometimes they wouldn't speak to me. Other times I heard them making fun of me. The most dreaded punishment came on nights when there was no light from the moon. Communist Father would say, "Go get some tender bamboo for the cow."

I was afraid to go outside after dark because very near the entrance to the house, the communist father's ancestors had built a cemetery. Many of his dead relatives were buried there. I was afraid that ghosts came out at night. Also, there was a little canal only about twenty steps away from the house. River shrimp and little animals lived in the water, and many things crept on the ground. All these creatures were very scary to me. I dreaded going outside in the pitch dark to get bamboo for the cow, but when told to do so, I knew I had to obey. I clearly remember such a night.

As I stepped out into the icy cold blackness of night, my weak legs shook. I crept along in total darkness. My straw shoes could not keep out the cold of the frozen ground. The fear inside my chest cut through me like I had swallowed a sharp rock. I tried to comfort myself by recalling the ghost stories Favorite Uncle used to tell me. I remembered how the children in the stories stood up to the ghosts. So I called out warnings, "Big Father is with me. Father and big, strong Brother are here. You cannot see them in the darkness, but Father and Brother will protect Double Luck."

I repeated these words and other brave warnings, but in my heart I knew they were not true. Communist Father and Brother would not protect me. Suddenly I thought about my dragon dream. I remembered how the great winged beast had swooped down, scooped me up, and taken me higher and higher. I wondered how fast a flying dragon could carry me to the bamboo trees, and before I knew it, my fingers were plucking branches. Soon my arms were full of tender bamboo. I remembered how it felt to soar above the earth, and without a single thought of ghosts, I practically flew back to the house.

Somehow I lived through the long, cold days on the porch and periodic trips to get bamboo on

moonless nights. Frostbitten feet and a deeply saddened heart were my worst scars. Looking back, it
was time that saved me—the changing seasons and
my own growth. There was an early spring that year,
and then came summer.

Along with summer came my first friends. Communist Father hired a lot of outsiders, young women,
who came to the area to find seasonal field work.
They pulled the wheat. After it dried, they separated
the straw from the wheat germ, which later could be
sold or exchanged for oil and rice and salty, double-
yolked duck eggs.

That summer, instead of keeping me locked out
of the house on the porch all day, my parents put me
to work. It was my job to put the straw and bamboo
in the stove and boil water in the wok and make tea.
I delivered the tea to the fields for the girls who
worked there. I got to know the workers, and they
just loved Double Luck. I told them stories of how
my parents died and how Sister-in-Law had sold me
to the Communist chief for five hundred pounds of
rice.

Sometimes we sang songs. Each village had its
own special song. One day I heard a woman singing
the song of my home village. *Oh, what joy!* I said to
myself, *This is a fortunate thing. This is a woman who
might know Sister.* I waited. Later, when we were
alone, I said to the woman from my own village,
"Oh, can you help me? After the harvest, when you
go home, will you take a message to my sister, Shiow
Jen? Tell her I am mistreated."

"I don't know your sister, but I will try," she said.

Too soon it seemed, the harvest was finished. As quickly as they had come, my new friends disappeared. I felt empty when they were gone, but I held on to the hope that my message, "Come and get me," would somehow reach Sister.

As the weather grew colder, so did my Communist parents. Communist Father said that because I was getting older, I needed harsher punishment. Almost daily there was a beating. On the nights when he went to Communist meetings, he left me home alone with Communist Mother. She didn't beat me; instead, she played tricks on me. Like a cat that toys with a mouse before eating it, Communist Mother tormented me. Looking back, the tricks she played were almost as painful as the beatings. It made my heart sick to know that they had grown to hate me so.

At the time, I didn't understand the things happening in the adult world. I was rarely taken out, and I couldn't read. I didn't know that China was weak from an eight-year war with Japan or that the Chinese Communist Party was taking over large parts of our country. I had my own personal struggles: getting enough to eat, staying warm in the winter, and keeping out of harm's way.

Toward the end of the year, Communist Father told Mother, "It is time Double Luck became a man. Tonight I will take him with me to the Communist meeting. We may have the makings of a great Communist here."

I didn't know what being a Communist meant, but as I marched along, like a soldier, I tried to stand tall. I held my shoulders square. It felt good to know I was going to become a man. With all my heart, I wanted to please Communist Father. *If I please him, I reasoned, he won't beat me so often.*

When we arrived at the community building, there must have been a hundred people there. Men, women field workers, and a few children were assembled in the basement. Father, the Communist chief of the village, stood in front of them all. I slipped in between two men in the front row where I could see Father standing under a huge picture of Mao Tse-tung. He began, "Comrades, the Chinese Communist Party is well established in the north and northeast."

As I watched him addressing the crowd, for the very first time, I realized I was part of something bigger than myself. I belonged to a race of people called Chinese. As simple as that thought is, at the time, to a young peasant boy, it seemed a great revelation. I lifted my chin and proudly gazed up at the big flag.

"The Nationalists have an advantage in numbers of men and weapons. They control a much larger area of land and have more people than we Communists, but they are exhausted by the long war with Japan. All of China is in turmoil."

A toothless man sitting next to me began stomping his feet. Then everyone cheered. *Why are they glad that China is in turmoil?* I wondered. I watched Communist Father's face closely.

"Our party membership has increased to many millions." As Communist Father spoke, he seemed to grow taller. He puffed out his chest and beat on the table with his fist. His face flushed red. "In the coming months, with minimal resistance, major cities will pass into Communist control."

Again everyone cheered and stomped their feet.

Communist Father lifted both his arms into the air and shouted, "Those who do not join the Chinese Communist Party will be shot. If you do not already belong, join tonight. Don't wait until it is too late. Teachers will be lined up and shot first."

"Teachers will be shot?" I asked out loud. But no one heard me. "Favorite Uncle is a teacher!" I yelled. Still no one listened to a little boy. Suddenly, somewhere outside, someone lit a string of firecrackers. I jumped. I thought it was gunfire and I was going to be shot right there in the basement.

Communist Father went on shaking his fists, his face sweating deeper shades of red. "The Chinese Communist Party will rule China without a fight. Because of this season's floods, millions of Chinese are homeless. Every day thousands of Chinese starve to death."

While the Communists stomped their feet and cheered wildly, those words burned like bamboo in my brain. *If thousands of people are starving,* I thought, *we have to help them. We have to get rice and take it to them. We cannot let our people starve to death.*

I was just a boy, but I knew how it felt to have an empty belly. I was not educated in matters of war, and I couldn't understand how people could cheer because others were starving and suffering. Were my family members who lived on the river homeless? I closed my eyes. I imagined Sister holding a crying baby over her head and wading through waist-deep water. *Maybe that is why Sister hasn't come after Chi Fa,* I thought.

Tears streamed down my face. I felt sick. I stumbled from the crowded room and ran breathlessly up the stairs. I heard Communist Father shout, "Soon all of China will be one—the Chinese Communist Party."

Everyone in the room applauded loudly.

Once outside, I gasped fresh air. Blinking tears from my eyes, I leaned up against the cold brick building to steady my weak knees. I could still hear his voice, but I could not make out his words—nor did I want to. I had heard enough. Realizing that terrible things were happening to the Chinese people, I felt overwhelmed with helplessness.

I crouched on the ground against the building. There was no moon to shed its light, and Heaven's net had pulled in all the stars except one. Gazing upward, I felt as alone as the single star that shone through the blackness. I wondered if Sister could see that same star. I wondered if she often thought about me. I tried to picture her face. I did not want to forget how she looked. Someday I would see Sister again, and I needed to be able to recognize her.

It had been more than a year since my uprooting, and for a young boy that is a very long time. The absence of my family was an ache that I lived with daily, but never had I felt the pain so sharply as I did at that very moment. I was confused about Communism and many other things, too, but one thing I knew for certain—I was lonely.

When the meeting was over, Communist Father found me and scolded me. "Double Luck, you are such a baby. I am ashamed to be seen with you."

He said I disgraced him by running out like a crybaby. "Waa waa," he mocked. "I don't want anyone to think you are my son. Don't walk beside me. Stay back." And he stalked off.

I stayed as far back as I could without losing sight of him, and like an obedient dog, I followed him home. I didn't want to, but I had nowhere else to go. I longed to be part of something good and strong. I wanted to go home to my own village—to my own family.

3
On the
Canal

(Be Persistent)

堅 韌

The summer of 1948, the year of the rat, was not like the wet summer before; the growing season was hot and dry. That season was a busy one. The women returned to the village and worked in the fields. Once again, it was my job to make and carry tea to the fields for the workers.

That summer's drought turned most fields into red dust. Fortunately for Communist Father, he owned a large wooden machine that pumped water from the canal and irrigated his fields. The pump worked when three or four people pedaled with their feet and turned a heavy wheel. It was hard work, but I liked being near the cool water with the women. As we pedaled, we told stories and sang songs. Always

I listened for the song of my home village so that I could ask about Sister or Favorite Uncle. Unfortunately, there were no women from my village among the workers that summer.

Despite the season's drought and the near famine it caused in our area, Communist parents had a good harvest. Later on, after the harvest, they needed to take a small portion of their wheat to another village to exchange it for rice. As luck would have it, they decided Double Luck should go along to help.

Communist Father told me to build a bamboo roof so that there would be shade on the boat. I liked cutting the bamboo branches and putting them over the top of the boat. It was the first time Communist Father had ever let me use his knife. When I finished, Communist Father and I lifted a wooden cart into the boat. Then we put five big bags of wheat into the boat. I felt strong helping to lift the heavy bags of wheat. I was glad to be going on the adventure, but I didn't let Communist Mother see my joy. I was certain that if she knew how much I wanted to go, she would make me stay home alone, locked outside on the porch.

The morning we were preparing to leave, I was so full of happiness I could hardly swallow my breakfast porridge. As we climbed onto the boat and drifted from shore, dawn broke with every shade of blue. I said to myself, *Surely I am favored by Heaven. Something wonderful is going to happen—I just know it!*

We drifted between the narrow canal banks thick with bamboo stalks shooting up many feet high. Like an orchestra of lutes, the bamboo leaves rustled in the wind. Never had I heard such sounds.

Communist Mother napped. Communist Father scribbled figures on paper so that he would be ready to make the best deals with his wheat. Late in the afternoon, when I grew very hungry, Communist Mother talked about the supper that could be bought in the marketplace. She said her favorites were salty, double-yolked duck eggs and sweet, ripe peaches.

"What do peaches and duck eggs taste like?" I asked Communist Father.

"Oh, Double Luck, you are such a stupid boy. You don't know anything," he scolded.

"I will tell you how they taste," said Communist Mother, smacking her lips. "A duck egg has a rich, buttery golden yolk that rests in a pearly bed of egg white. Peaches are pink and yellow and juicy and taste sweeter than candy."

My stomach rumbled at the thought of such delicious foods. I could hardly wait for supper.

At sunset we reached a spot where Communist Father wanted to pull the boat to shore. "There!" He pointed to a place ahead. With his hand he motioned for me to jump out of the boat and pull it ashore.

I could not swim, but I had to obey. Holding the edge of the boat, I slipped into the cold water. Fortunately the water was only waist deep. I dug my toes into the gooey mud to get a good grip and gave the little boat a hard shove. It drifted exactly where Communist Father had pointed. I felt proud as I waded to shore. First I helped him lift the heavy cart out of the boat. Then, one at a time, we carried the bags of wheat to the cart. Hungry and eager for a ripe peach and a duck egg, I grabbed the cart's handles.

Communist Mother called to me, "Double Luck, where do you think you are going?"

"To the marketplace," I said.

"No! You are soaking wet. Stay here and guard the boat. Father will eat your duck egg, and I will eat an extra peach for you."

With those few words, it was settled. There would be no supper for Double Luck.

Communist Father took the cart handles from me and gave the cart a shove. Soon he and Communist Mother disappeared through the bamboo opening. I stood and listened to the wooden wheels rumbling along the hard-packed earth. Then I got into the boat and blinked away my tears. I was hungry, but I had gone without supper before. I curled up in the bottom of the boat. It was very uncomfortable. *Tomorrow,* I told myself, *I will make a bed with bamboo leaves.* I tucked a bent arm under my head for a pillow, and then I fell asleep.

That night, lulled by the rocking of the boat, I dreamed that I rode on the back of my mighty dragon. We soared to a place where Sister and my whole family were picnicking on the green grass. When the dragon landed, Sister and everyone ran up to greet me. They told me how handsome I had grown. Then we sat on the grass, all talking at once. We ate ripe peaches and duck eggs until our bellies were too full to hold another bite. It was a wonderful dream.

The next morning, while it was still dark, the crowing of a flock of birds awoke me. Sadly, I realized it had only been a dream. I was not with Sister and family. I was alone. I was famished, and there was nothing to eat. When dawn's light broke, I discovered that I had slept next to a great cemetery. It was on the side of a mountain that rose beyond the bamboo wall. Had I known the cemetery was so close, I would have been afraid to fall asleep for fear of the ghosts. I hoped Communist parents would come back before dark. Just in case, I busied myself making a bed of bamboo leaves in the bottom of the boat. I made a thick pile so that it would be soft.

I couldn't see through the bamboo tree wall, and that first morning, not a single person came down the canal road. It didn't occur to me to go beyond the bamboo trees. My thinking was this: *I had been told to guard the boat, and I had to obey.*

When the sun was blazing overhead, I used my cupped hands to scoop up water. I drank and drank. Then I found a piece of bark shaped like a little bowl. I scooped up more water in the bark bowl and set it in the sun to warm. Later I crushed some dried bamboo leaves and sprinkled them in the warm water and stirred it with a little stick. When it looked like tea, I drank it. It tasted good, but still I was shaking with hunger.

When the sky sparkled with stars, I climbed into

the boat and lay down on my bamboo-leaf bed. Hungry and afraid of the ghosts in the cemetery, I cried myself to sleep. That night I didn't even have the comfort of a dragon dream. Instead I had nightmares that hungry birds pecked at my belly.

When dawn finally brought a new day, hopelessness blew through me like an angry wind. Two whole days without food—I was dizzy and weak. My stomach and head both ached. "How long can I live without food before I starve to death?" I asked out loud. I sat in the boat and watched the rising sun streak the sky with soft yellow and pink light, and I wondered how many ripe peaches Communist Mother had eaten.

When the sun rose above the mountaintop, I waded to shore. I used my hands to scoop some water and drank it. Then I sat in the shade and waited. In the middle of the day, I saw something a long way off. I couldn't tell what it was. It was as wide as it was tall. Whatever it was, I hoped it couldn't swim. I waded to the boat and got in, where I felt safer.

I watched as it came nearer. When it got closer, I realized it was a woman with a great load of sticks on her back. I jumped out of the boat and waded back to shore. Dizzy from hunger, I ran up to the woman. "I have not eaten in two days," I sobbed.

The woman told me, "My dear child, we all face difficult times. There was a drought this summer. There is no wheat, no rice, no food. You're not special. I, too, am very hungry."

But I didn't give up. She was my only hope. Without a single thought of guarding the boat, I followed her through the opening in the wall of bamboo. She was stooped from the heavy load on her back, but still she moved at a quick pace. I walked beside her, telling her my stories. I told her how I had been sold to the Communist chief for five hundred pounds of rice and how the parents mistreated me.

"Don't waste your breath. Don't walk any farther because I can't provide any kind of food or anything for you." Then, pointing a long finger in the direction from where we had come, she said, "Go away!"

"But I am starving," I told the woman again.

Bending to pick up sticks as I saw them and adding them to her load, I kept perfect pace with her. After a great distance, we came to a big, fine house. She knocked on the back door. We waited for what seemed like a very long time, until a man opened the door. He was the oldest man I had ever seen. He was stooped as if he, too, had a load of sticks on his back, but he didn't. As he shuffled off the porch, both his white beard and braid dragged in the dust.

The very old man and I began unloading the sticks from the woman's back and neatly stacking them near the door. As we worked, the woman briefly told the ancient one my story. She said, "This little child has walked with me for quite some time, and he hasn't eaten for a couple of days."

The man shook his head. His slits for eyes opened slightly. He peered at me through thick lashes and asked, "You have not eaten in two days?"

I shook my head. "Almost three days," I told him.

"This boy must not go hungry another hour," said the very old man.

As soon as the sticks were stacked, he led us into his kitchen. Two headless, plucked chickens dangled upside down from a hook attached to the ceiling. In one corner stood seven big jars. *This is a very rich man,* I said to myself. Without looking, I knew the big jars held rice, flour, and cakes. In China, in good times, when people have plenty of wheat, they grind the whole wheat into flour and make great stacks of cakes. They fry the cakes in a pan for a few minutes, then put them outside, under the sun, to dry. When the cakes are completely dried, they are stored in big jars. If there is an emergency or they need food quickly, they pull out a few cakes, put them in boiling water, and that is their meal.

The ancient one put water on the stove to boil. He opened one big jar and took out some cakes. These he dropped one cake at a time into the boiling water. Soon he had piled high two bowls with cakes. He shoved the bowls in front of us and said, "Eat."

Between bites of cake I asked, "Where am I? What is the name of this village?"

His answer pleased me very much. "This is Mao Cho Wei," he said.

"Mao Cho Wei! This is my village," I said. "I am home and I didn't even know it." I was so happy I could hardly swallow. I asked the old man and woman if either of them knew my sister, Shiow Jen. They did not know Sister.

"Favorite Uncle is a teacher," I said. "Do you know my uncle?"

Neither knew Uncle, but the old man remembered my father and my father's father—owners of the village store. "All dead," he said, making a circle in the air with his hand, "and that, of course, cannot help you today."

He rose and put more water on the stove. "You look just like your father's father. Did anyone ever tell you that?"

"No," I said. I was grateful to hear that news.

"Your father and grandfathers knew how to live good and simple lives. They were honorable men." Then he went on to tell me about my older brother, Ching Fa, losing the store to gambling debts— which, of course, I already knew. "Too much rice wine made him slow-witted as an old woman," he said.

I did not comment on Brother's intelligence or lack of intelligence. By not speaking, I could save face for my family and still honor the old one who had given me so many cakes and such good news about where I was. When we finished eating every crumb of the cakes, the very old man gave us rice tea. I thanked him. I asked if he had a job that I could do to repay him.

"In caring for others, I am serving heaven," he said. "I only offer you what I would want you to offer me if I were standing in your shoes." He looked at my bare feet and said, "Pity, pity. Such a good boy, and no father to appreciate him."

He walked us to the door. He gave the woman some coins for the sticks. Combing his beard with his fingers, he said to me, "Remember, it is far better to be a young man with an empty belly than an old man with a full belly." Then he closed the door.

Outside, the woman squeezed my hand. "Dear boy, we live not as we wish or dream, but as we must. I hope that you find your sister. May good fortune find you."

She pointed a long finger in the direction I should go to get back to the boat, and then walked off in the opposite direction, bending to pick up sticks as she went.

On my way back to the boat, I became disoriented. I saw a crowd of men talking. Hoping to get help, I went up to them. "I am trying to get back to the canal," I said. "Which way should I go?"

One man rudely shoved me away and said, "Don't waste our time! We have important things to do."

I stood outside the circle of men and listened as they spoke of the Chinese Communist takeover. The man who had pushed me said, "The Communists have already taken over many of the small villages along the river. Soon they will move into the bigger cities. Because we are educated, they will shoot us first."

Another man read the names of villagers who had most recently joined the Communist Party.

"Traitors," said one man. "The Chinese people are like separate grains of sand. They never stick together. The Chinese are too willing to be led. Mao and the Chinese Communist Party are going to take over this country, and there is nothing we can do to stop them."

"Pity," said an old man whose beard reached his knees. "You do not know whom you can trust these days. Everywhere there are spies. That might even be a spy there—that boy!" he said, pointing a crooked finger at me.

For a second I liked the idea that the men thought I was important enough to be a spy. Each face turned. They stared at me. A man with great gaps between his teeth shoved me to the ground. "Get out of here! Go away, spy," he hissed. Another man kicked dirt at me.

"I am a boy, not a spy," I said, scrambling to my feet and rushing off. Glancing over my shoulder, I saw the men scattering. Not knowing if I was going in the right direction, I walked and walked. Soon I was hopelessly lost.

After a while I heard a little noise, like the sound that a hummingbird makes. I turned, and there was a little boy, just barely old enough to walk. He was naked except for a little red apron covering his front. A soft, golden light surrounded him. I was drawn to the boy, so as he toddled, I followed. A calmness swept over me as I trailed along in his footsteps. I followed him for about the time it would take to boil water. Then, in the blink of an eye, he vanished. One second he was there, the next second he was gone.

Looking around, I realized that I had followed him deep into a cemetery. My first thought was that the boy had been an evil ghost or spirit who had lured me into the clutches of death. I stared and spun full circle. With nothing at my back, I had no protection from whatever horror might snatch me. A sob rocked me. Afraid to let crying cloud my vision, I used all my willpower to dam my tears. I could feel a ring of invisible beings closing in on me. I had to run, but I could not get my legs to work.

"Save me!" I whispered. And at that instant, I remembered I was in my home village. My parents were buried in this cemetery. For some reason, that thought brought me comfort. I crouched and touched the red soil. "Papa, Mama," I cried aloud, "it is me, Chi Fa. I am grown up now." I stood. "See how big I have grown? I am nearly eight years old. I am a good boy. I have lived with Communist Father and Mother for two years. I have learned the Chinese way: swallow pain—let sadness feed the soul."

After saying these words, I felt a stillness settle around me. If there were ghosts, they were only people who had lived and died. Ghosts would have no reason to harm a little boy. "Mama, Papa," I said, "I need to find my way back to the boat. I need to find Sister. Help me." With these words, I found my legs could walk again. Rather than rushing down-hill, I summoned the courage to climb farther uphill in search of a view of the valley below.

I climbed to a spot where I could see the arrow-straight canal in the valley and spotted the boat, a speck on the water. I pointed myself in the right direction and hurried downhill. As the light of day dimmed, a thick fog rolled up the hill and met me halfway. By the time I reached the canal, I could barely see my feet. I listened for the water lapping against the side of the boat and waded into it. I crawled into the boat, where deep sleep engulfed me.

I awoke at dawn feeling brave. After washing my face and feet in the canal, I sat in the early sunlight to dry. Shortly, I saw a man walking up the canal road. As he came closer, I could clearly see that it was Favorite Uncle. Filled with joy, I ran into his arms. I said, "Uncle, this is great luck seeing you here."

"It is not *luck* that brought me here, Chi Fa," he said with a smile. "An old woman selling sticks came to the school. She told me where I could find you."

"I want to go home with you, Uncle," I pleaded.

"Oh, no, I am sorry, Chi Fa, but I cannot take you. You belong to the Communist chief. If I steal you away, he would have me arrested. You belong to him."

"They are mean to me, Uncle. They beat me. They starve me."

"I am sorry for you, Chi Fa," said Uncle.

"And their ancestors are buried in the front yard, Uncle. I was afraid of the ghosts. In the winter, when there was no moonlight, they sent me to get tender bamboo for the cow. I remembered what you taught me, and I tried to be brave, but, Uncle, I was so afraid. Please don't let them take me back."

"It is good that you remembered to be brave, Chi Fa. You will grow to be very strong. Try to make the best of your situation. Someday you will be a man, and then you can make your own future. I cannot help you, because you are his son."

"But I want to be your son, Uncle. He does not treat me like I am his son. They both treat me like I am a dog—a bad dog. I want to live in my own village, near my family. I can work, Uncle. I can work in your kitchen. I know how to build a fire and make tea and carry it to the fields." As I pleaded, tears gushed from my eyes.

"You are young. Be brave. Have faith in yourself," said Uncle. "I should not even be here talking to you. I have to go now."

It was no use trying to convince him. He was afraid to help me because of Communist Father's title. Besides, Uncle was poor. He couldn't be responsible for another mouth to feed. He didn't have the energy to stand up to anyone. I wanted Uncle to be brave, like the children in his stories, but he could not.

"Okay," I told him, "if you cannot help me, please go get Sister. I want to see her before I go. Tell her where I am. Tell her I am waiting here to see her. Will you do that, Uncle? Please!"

He didn't promise, but he patted my head. Then he and his worried face were gone.

The rest of the warm morning, I sat in the boat, hoping to see Sister's face before going back with the Communist parents. I shifted my eyes back and forth between the opening in the bamboo where Communist parents would return and the canal road where I hoped Sister would appear. I thought about hiding in the bamboo until the Communist parents came back and left in their boat, but I knew Uncle was right—they could make trouble for my family. I decided the only thing to do was to stay in the boat.

When the sun made very short shadows, Sister came. I knew her from afar. I waved until my arm felt like it was falling off. I ran to her—my new hope. I wept. Sister wept. We held each other. The only sound was our sobs. I didn't ever want to let go of her.

Wiping away her tears, Sister handed me a little tin box with rice and vegetables and two shrimp inside. I dried my eyes with my hand and began to eat. Between bites, I told Sister how the Communist parents mistreated me. I showed her my scars. I told her about eating the sweet rice cakes and Communist Father hanging me by my hair. I said, "Sister, he beats me and calls me names. Communist Mother plays tricks on me." I told her everything. "I kept my promise, Sister. I never forgot that I was a good boy."

She gave me a hug, and we cried again. She held

me close and rocked me in her arms. She sang the song she used to sing to me when I was a baby.

Row, row, row to sea.
Grandma's on the bridge.
Grandma calls to me,
"What a good baby."

The red sky of sunset brought the Communist parents back with their cart of rice and bellies full of eggs and peaches. Communist Father staggered a bit.

Seeing me talking to an adult, Communist Father flashed me a mean look. But Sister was brave. With her arms folded across her chest, she walked up to them and said, "I am Chi Fa's sister."

Communist Mother put on the face of a dog getting ready to bite its enemy. She pointed her finger at me and growled, "You miserable little worm. We treated you so well. What did you expect? We paid five hundred pounds of rice for you. We own you."

"We trained you to be our son, you ungrateful little devil," added Communist Father.

Sister stepped closer to the Communist parents. "My little brother has been mistreated by you. You may be the Communist chief of your village and have a little bit of power, but I will report you to a higher authority. Let my brother go. If you refuse to let him go, there will be trouble."

Communist parents moved to one side and spoke privately. Communist Father waved his arms

wildly as Communist Mother shook her finger in his
face. Then they stood silently, looking at each other
for a long while.

Sister's footsteps broke the silence. Walking up
to them again, she asked, "What is your decision?"

Communist Father spoke first, "Take him. I don't
want him. He is a big disappointment to me."

"He eats too much, and he is lazy," snapped
Communist Mother.

"Then it is settled," said Sister. "Chi Fa will come
with me."

"Get out of my sight, you ungrateful worm,"
barked Communist Mother.

"Go!" commanded Communist Father, pointing
up the canal road.

"One more thing," said Sister. After a long pause,
she added, "I will need rice."

"Rice?" snapped Communist Mother.

"Yes, rice," said Sister.

"Rice?" growled Communist Father.

"Rice—to silence me about the abuse Chi Fa has
suffered," Sister stated calmly.

I had never seen Communist Mother so furious.
She lunged toward Sister. I thought she might grab
Sister's hair or claw at her eyes, but Communist
Father stopped her with a look. He spoke to her with
his eyes. Finally he turned to Sister and gave her a
very small nod.

Sister indicated with one pointed finger for me to
take the cart with two bags of rice. Weak-kneed, I
walked over and lifted the heavy cart's handles. I

gave the cart a little shove and pushed it onto the canal road. Together we walked off. Never in my life have I felt as tall as I did pushing my cart of rice. I was free. I was rich. I had enough rice to feed a boy for two years. And Sister's arm around my shoulder told me that I was loved. This was the happiest hour of my childhood.

We walked with our chins up and our heads held high. Above, a sky full of stars twinkled for us. *Surely I have good fortune,* I told myself. "I am proud of you, Sister," I said as we moved along the canal road.

"I am proud of you, too, Chi Fa," said Sister.

4
Favorite Uncle's House
(Be Considerate)

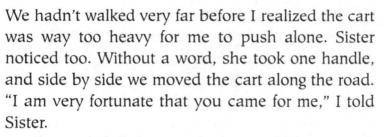

We hadn't walked very far before I realized the cart was way too heavy for me to push alone. Sister noticed too. Without a word, she took one handle, and side by side we moved the cart along the road. "I am very fortunate that you came for me," I told Sister.

She smiled. "Chi Fa is lucky. Good fortune will find you."

Rescued from the Communist parents and going home to my own village, I believed those words with all my heart.

As we walked along beneath the star-filled sky, Sister talked about her babies. "Chi Haw was very disappointed when Daughter Number One was born because he wanted a son. Since then, two more babies—both girls. But this time," said Sister, stopping to take a rest and patting her round belly, "I will have a son for Chi Haw."

I did not know what to say to her.

"Daughters are very noisy. It is a good thing Chi Haw is deaf." Sister laughed, though her face was sad. Then she lowered her voice. Almost whispering, she said, "Every day Chi Haw grows more bitter and more difficult to please."

"I will help take care of the little girls," I promised Sister.

Turning her eyes from me, Sister said, "I am sorry, Chi Fa, but you may not live with us."

"I can work, Sister. I will help you," I begged.

"No. Chi Haw has forbidden me to bring you home," said Sister.

"Why does he hate me?" I asked.

"You are a bitter reminder to him that he has no son of his own," said Sister.

"I could have been his son," I told her.

"To Chi Haw, it is not the same," said Sister.

"If I cannot live with you, where will I go?" I asked.

Sister took both handles of the cart and pushed it up the road. The noise of the wheels on the road made it difficult to hear her plan: "Tonight you will come home with me. Tomorrow I will take you to Favorite Uncle's house."

"Aunt doesn't want me, either," I told Sister, catching up to her.

"You have rice. Aunt will be glad to take a boy

who has a cart full of rice. They are very poor, and you will be their good fortune."

After that, neither of us spoke. There was nothing else to say.

By the time the moon had risen, we were at Sister's back door. Chi Haw was up and drinking tea in the kitchen. The lines on his face told me he was worried and sad. He did not even nod; he just stared past me. When he finished his tea, he gave Sister a look and then went to bed.

After Sister fed me sticky rice, she took me to the bedroom where I had slept years before. There, her sleeping girls were lined up, like tiny mice, in the straw bed. "They are beautiful," I told her. "Beautiful treasures."

With pride, Sister bowed her head, and then, wearily, she led me to the courtyard, where she unrolled a mat on the floor. She handed me a quilt. "It has been a long day," she said. "Get some sleep, Chi Fa."

"Thank you, Sister," I said. "Good night."

So tired I could barely draw a breath, I tucked my bent arm under my head and curled up in a tight little ball. I thought back to the last time I had slept in this house. So much had happened in four years. Somewhere in the distance I heard a cricket's welcome-home song: "Chi Fa. Chi Fa."

The next morning I opened my eyes and saw three little girls peeking around the wall at me. They giggled.

"Come here," I said. "I am your uncle. I am

Uncle Chi Fa." I liked the way it sounded—*Uncle Chi Fa*. I felt very grown up.

They did not come to me. Instead, two ran and one crawled off to the kitchen. I followed.

Chi Haw was not in the kitchen. "Gone for the day," said Sister.

After breakfast I helped Sister draw buckets of water from the well. We carried them outside and watered three trees. Each tree was a different size, like stepping stones. "They are peach trees, with strong and deep roots," Sister said proudly.

As we watered the trees, Sister explained that each time she had a little girl, she planted a peach seed. In the Chinese culture, peaches are the symbol for long life. Sister wanted her little girls to have long, happy lives. "From the oldest tree, nearly four years old now, I picked several baskets of peaches this year," she told me with a smile.

"What are peaches like?" I asked.

"Very good and sweet," said Sister, "like my little girls. Today you will taste ripe peaches as part of your welcome-home supper. And I have duck eggs, too. Do you like duck eggs?"

"Duck eggs? I do not know, Sister. I have never tasted peaches or duck eggs."

"Oh, Chi Fa," said Sister. "I am sorry for you."

Chi Haw did not come home at all that day. In the early evening, Sister stir-fried many tiny river shrimp with ginger and leeks. She made sticky rice and boiled large duck eggs. For dessert we ate sweet,

juicy peaches. Never had I tasted anything so delicious as a peach. As my thoughts drifted back to
Communist Mother, I shivered. Just the thought of
her gave me a chill.

After we washed and put away the dishes, Sister,
her little girls, and I started for Favorite Uncle's
house. Just as she had done so many years before,
Sister glided along the dusty road with hurried steps.
This time she pushed my cart of rice with a baby on
top. "Don't mind Aunt. She is cranky. Uncle cares
for you and wants you in his house. Promise me you
will be strong and patient."

"I promise," I said.

Holding one hand of each of my other two nieces,
I tried to close the gap between the girls and their
mother. Soon we were there. Unlike the first time I
was dropped on Uncle's doorstep, Sister didn't hurry
off. While the little girls and I waited outside, she
went inside and talked with Aunt and Favorite
Uncle. Shortly, Aunt came to the door and made a
motion with her hand for me to come closer. "You
may stack the bags of rice on the floor in the
kitchen," she said.

Favorite Uncle patted my head. "Hello, Chi Fa."

Uncle helped me carry in the two bags of rice.
We put them where Aunt directed. Aunt looked the
same, except her belly was a bit bigger. My cousins
had grown. Girl Cousin was pretty and very nice,
like Uncle. Boy Cousin looked like Aunt—the same
flaring nostrils. I thought, *Pity to look like Aunt.*

We all sat in the kitchen in the glow of the lantern light. Uncle asked me to share with them what it had been like to live with the Communist parents. "Tell us a story," he said.

I did not want to speak of the many cruel things that had happened to me. I thought, *Little girls should not hear about such things.* So I said, "Uncle, you tell better stories. Please, Uncle, won't you tell us a ghost story?"

"Yes, yes," said two of my nieces, clapping.

"Please, Papa," urged Girl Cousin.

So Favorite Uncle began his story. Wide-eyed, the little ones listened while Uncle told of a little boy who was sent out in the darkness, through a cemetery, to get tender bamboo for a cow. He said the boy was very brave. When he got to the part where the little boy yelled out to the ghosts, the little girls joined in: "Go away, bad ghosts! Never come back!"

I listened to the story and watched the faces of my nieces and cousin. I hoped they would never have to yell at ghosts or experience fear and pain. *Little girls should never have to be afraid,* I thought, *and neither should little boys.*

After that first night, Favorite Uncle didn't tell any more stories. He wasn't his happy self. Preoccupied with the Communist takeover of China and worried about his own safety, Uncle hardly noticed the abuse I took from Aunt and Boy Cousin.

By the spring of 1949, the year of the ox, I had been living in the house of my uncle for six long months. On each of those days, I got less than a mouthful of my own rice. Every day, just before Aunt served supper, she would tell me, "Oh, Chi Fa, go to the pigpen and feed the pigs. Hurry back. It is almost time to eat."

Always I would go, and when I returned, the rice would be gone. "Oh, Chi Fa, so sorry. I forgot about you. I will get you something else to eat."

Aunt pretended to apologize in front of Uncle, but after Uncle left the kitchen, what she would feed me was pigs' food. Day after day it was the same thing. She'd beat up sweet potatoes—not the whole, big sweet potatoes, but the little undeveloped ones that had no nutrients. They were nothing more than stringy roots. Once she tried to feed me the part of the wheat that is separated from the germ and is usually thrown away. It was too tough to chew or swallow. "May I have a little rice, too?" I asked politely.

"Chi Fa! Ungrateful boy! Don't you know that many are hungry? There's not enough food in China. Every day thousands of Chinese people die of starvation. We take you in, we give you a place to sleep and food to eat, and still you are not happy. Complain, complain, complain," scolded Aunt.

I pushed the plate of wheat husks away. "I am not hungry," I lied.

Each day I grew thinner and thinner. I was always hungry, but no one ever beat me or hung me by my hair, so it was better than what I had been used to. Many nights during those months at Favorite Uncle's, I had dragon dreams, which drew my mind from the things that troubled me.

Unlike the previous spring, that year there was plenty of rain. The fields were green with growing wheat. But because many people in China were starving, food in the fields was not safe. Hungry peasants often stripped fields clean. That was how it came about that Boy Cousin and I were given the job of guarding Favorite Uncle's two wheat fields. He built us a little tent near the fields so that we could listen at night. Aunt gave us one little blanket to share.

Early one morning, while it was still very cold and dark, I heard Cousin groan, "Give me the cover." Then he kicked me and yanked the blanket.

His fat should keep him warm, I thought. So I took one corner of the blanket and gave it a tug.

"Stop!" yelled Cousin, "or I will beat you up." And with that he gave the blanket another yank, leaving me completely uncovered.

"Share the blanket," I told Cousin. But he did not give me back part of the blanket, so I took one corner again and gave it another good yank.

Cousin jumped up and started whirling his fists in the air, screaming, "Come on! You want to fight me for the blanket? Get up, you little skinny worm."

I did not want to fight, so I did not get up. Cousin kicked me in the side. Hard. "Afraid to fight?" he snorted.

Yes, I was afraid to fight him. He was much bigger than I was. "It would be shameful for you to beat on someone half your size. What would it prove?" I asked him.

Cousin was nearly eleven and built big like Aunt. I could not fight and win against him. I was little and thin, too weak to wrestle for the blanket. I just lay there shivering until it was time to get up and do my chores.

Later that same day, I heard from Favorite Uncle that Sister had a new baby girl. So as soon as I had finished my chores, I walked to her house. I found her on her knees in the garden, planting another peach seed. I knew she wanted a baby boy. I did not know what to say to her.

"I have another beautiful treasure," said Sister. "Come see."

Sister washed her hands at the well, and then she took me into her kitchen to show me the new baby. The tiny baby was sleeping in a basket that hung at the end of a rope dangling from the ceiling.

"She is pretty," I said.

"She looks like you, Chi Fa. When you were a baby, you looked just like her," said Sister.

"Did I have a nose so small?" I asked.

Sister laughed. The baby began to cry. Sister used one hand to gently rock the basket back and forth and the other hand to make me onion cakes and tea. As she worked, she sang.

Row, row, row to sea.
Grandma's on the bridge.
Grandma calls to me,
"What a good baby."

She asks, "How is Baby's mama?"
She asks, "How is Baby's papa?"

When she finished her song, I asked Sister, "Where is Chi Haw?"

"He has gone to visit his family," she said. "He will be back in a few days or a week. Always Chi Haw comes home."

I thought about Sister's four little treasures. How could such sweetness come from that wrinkled, bitter man? *Like peaches from a peach seed,* I told myself.

"Why have you come, Little Brother? What do you want to say?" Sister asked.

"I am sorry to complain; you have your own sorrows," I told her.

"Never mind my sorrows. What do you want to tell me, Chi Fa?"

"Well," I began, "Aunt doesn't give me enough to eat. Cousin won't share the blanket at night. Day after day I'm hungry and cold."

She didn't answer for a while. Then, putting a plate of onion cakes in front of me, she sternly warned, "Chi Fa, Uncle's house is the only hope you have."

Poking onion cake into my mouth, I gazed pitifully at Sister.

"I see that you are sometimes hungry, but you are not tortured or beaten like you were when you were with the Communist parents. It's better than your previous circumstances. I advise you not to make a fuss."

"Sister," I said, "let me live with you. I will work hard. I will earn my keep. Can't you see that I am starving?"

"I see that you are swallowing your onion cakes without chewing, and you are talking with a stuffed mouth," scolded Sister.

I did not say anything more. I just ate my onion cakes. As I chewed, Sister studied my arms and legs. After what seemed like a long time, she stood and hurried from the room. Shortly, she returned carrying a beautiful quilt. "This will keep you warm," she said, handing me the bundle. "Mother made it just before she died. I was saving it for your wedding day, but you need it now. Mama would want you to have it today."

I could hardly believe my great fortune. A warm quilt of my own! "Sister," I said, "you make me very happy."

"Good. I like to see my little brother happy. Now go, before Aunt thinks you are here complaining to me," she said, shooing me away as if I were a fly.

The sky was empty except for the big yellow sun sinking behind the hills. All the way back to Favorite Uncle's house, I wondered what I should say when Aunt asked me about the quilt. The voice inside my heart told me to say as little as possible.

When I went into the kitchen, Aunt was cooking four small fish and some sticky rice. She took one look at my quilt and said, "So, Chi Fa went to see Sister."

"I wanted to see the new baby," I said truthfully.

"Another girl! That makes Chi Haw very happy to have many little girls in his house," teased Aunt.

"Baby is beautiful. Sister is very happy," I told her.

"Happy? Huh!" said Aunt. Then, grabbing at my quilt, she asked, "Is this for me? A present from Shiow Jen because I take such good care of her little brother?"

"No," I said, stepping back. "This is mine. Mama made it."

"That is your quilt?" asked Cousin, coming into the kitchen. He put his dirty hand into the pot of sticky rice and grabbed fingers full. "Looks girlish."

Aunt swatted at Cousin's fingers with a chopstick, but she missed. She always missed. Every day Aunt pretended Boy Cousin was not allowed to taste the food she was cooking, but he always did. He sampled more food before supper than I ate at supper. "Stop that, Baby," she said.

She called him Baby. And he was a baby—a big baby.

Uncle came into the kitchen. "What a beautiful quilt," he said. "That was made by my sister. I recognize the pattern. Your grandmother taught your mother how to make that kind of quilt when she was your age, Chi Fa."

"It is almost suppertime," interrupted Aunt. "Chi Fa, hurry out and feed the pigs." She pointed to a big tub of sweet potato roots.

I put my quilt on top of my sleeping mat, then lifted the heavy tub and carried it outside. I heard her calling after me, "Hurry, so you won't miss supper."

I smiled to myself. Aunt did not know that already Sister had filled my belly with many onion cakes and tea. I did not even want the sticky rice that Cousin's dirty fingers had touched.

When Cousin and I went to the field that night, the full moon was alone in the sky—not a cloud or star was shining. I knew it would be cold by morning. Before we crawled into the little tent, Cousin unrolled his thin blanket, held it up, and said, "I am glad I have my blanket all to myself now."

"Me too," I said.

"Aren't you ashamed to sleep under such a quilt? It looks like a lady's fancy gown," he teased.

"No, Cousin, I am proud of my quilt. Red is my favorite color. It is full of batting and will keep me warm."

He snatched the quilt from my hands and wrapped two corners around his shoulders. Pretending to be a fancy lady, he danced around, humming a stupid tune. One edge dragged in the dirt, but I did not try to get it back for fear a scuffle would rip it. Instead, I just watched. Since his mother was not there to laugh and cheer him on, Cousin's prank wasn't fun for long. Soon he grew bored with the game and tossed my quilt to the ground.

"Not a man's blanket. I'm glad I do not have to sleep under your quilt. You may have it all to yourself. I do not want to share it with you," said Cousin.

"That is too bad, Cousin, because it is a wide quilt. It would cover us both, and we'd still have lots of quilt to tuck in on the sides. Two covers on top of two boys would make each boy doubly warm," I told him.

"If I were a baby, or blind and could not see the quilt, I would not mind its warmth. But I am a man, and a man does not sleep under such a thing."

Sometimes I was sure Cousin's mouth said the opposite of what his heart felt. To myself I said, *Cousin wants a fine quilt like this, too.*

I went inside the tent and unrolled my mat and lay down. Carefully I spread the quilt over me and pulled it up over my head so that I wouldn't have to listen to Cousin telling me what a "big man" he was. "Good night, Cousin," I said.

He did not answer.

In the middle of the night, a cold wind rocked our little tent. I heard Cousin's teeth chattering, and I felt him pulling on my quilt. When he had enough of the quilt over him, he tucked it in along the edge of his body. The next morning, Cousin pretended he did not notice that the quilt was over both of us.

We never spoke of the quilt again. Each night was the same. After he thought I was sleeping, Cousin would pull one edge of my quilt over his shivering body. I didn't always like Cousin, but still, a boy should not have to freeze. Besides, a fat boy puts off a lot of body heat. Sleeping under Mama's quilt with Cousin was like sleeping next to a potbellied stove.

5
Grandma's Hut
(Be Thankful)

One evening when the sky was full of moon, Sister and her four little girls came to Uncle's house. In a flurry, Sister rushed into the kitchen. "I have news," she said cheerfully. "I have found a good job for Chi Fa. He will be living with another family, where he will be the kitchen help. It is only a few blocks away. You may still see Chi Fa whenever you like."

"Huh," Aunt snorted. "He will no longer help guard the fields and feed the pigs? Ungrateful, that is what he is!"

Uncle lowered his eyes and did not speak, but I thought I saw a small smile cross his lips.

"So sorry," said Sister, "but this is what is best for Chi Fa."

The matter was closed. Sister had spoken.

"Will Uncle tell us a story?" asked one of the little girls.

"No time for stories," said Sister. "Chi Fa, get your quilt and come with me."

Uncle patted my head. Then Sister, her girls, and I were on the road. Even with a baby in her arms, Sister moved quickly. With hurried steps, she glided along the road ahead of me. "Be helpful," she advised. "The woman who you will be living with is very old and kind. She will feed you. You will be warm."

"Oh, thank you, Sister," I said.

"And remember, Chi Fa, you are lucky. Good fortune will find you."

Sister didn't have time to give me many more wise words, because soon we stopped at a round hut with a big straw roof. It was a strange sight. Weeds grew up everywhere, and a little lamb was tethered in the yard. It had chewed the weeds to the ground inside the circle where the rope allowed it to travel. Looking closer I saw the whole yard was a garden—a garden without rows. Flowers and wild onions and garlic sprang up every which way. The aroma was wonderful. Vegetable plants, flowering and budding, crowded the yard.

Sister told the little girls to wait in the yard.

"May we pet the lamb?" they begged.

"Yes, pet the lamb," she said. Then she went to the doorway of the hut and called out. "I have brought the boy. I am here with Chi Fa."

A tiny, stooped, ancient woman with wispy white hair came to the doorway. "This is your brother?" she asked.

"Yes, this is Chi Fa," Sister said proudly.

"Welcome, Chi Fa." The woman's wide smile was sweet, and the twinkle in her eyes told me she was glad I was there. She grabbed my hand and squeezed it hard. "Oh, dear, you are very thin. Are you hungry?" she asked. And not waiting for an answer, she took Mama's quilt from my arms and placed it on one of two big straw beds.

I looked at Sister to see if I should say that I was hungry. When I did not speak, Sister answered for me. "Chi Fa is a growing boy. He is always hungry."

"Very good!" said the old woman. "I like hungry boys. I have two of my own. We are not rich, but we have plenty to eat."

She went to her stove in the center of the room and scooped rice and vegetables from a big black wok and put them into a bowl. She placed the bowl of warm food on the table. "Sit and eat," she said, handing me chopsticks. She poured tea with a toasty aroma into a cup and placed it next to the bowl of food. "Drink," she said.

I lifted the cup to my lips with thankfulness. The warm tea felt like silk on my tongue and mouth and throat. I could not remember ever tasting such a rich flavor.

"That is lima-bean-shell tea. I grew the beans and shelled them. I dried the shells in the sun and then toasted them in the wok," said the old woman. "Do you like it?"

Letting the richness find its way to my stomach, I said, "Oh, yes, very much."

As I began to eat the rice and vegetables, two men came into the hut. "These are my little boys," the woman told me. "This is Chi Fa," she told the men. "Chi Fa has come to stay."

Like Sister telling Aunt, "Chi Fa is going," the old woman told her sons, "Chi Fa is staying." It was settled. Nothing left to be said.

With trembling hands, the old woman poured tea into chipped cups. Placing a finger just below the inside rim of each cup, she stopped pouring when the tea touched it. I then realized that she was nearly blind. Everyone sat around the big table, sipping the delicious tea. I looked at Sister and the old woman. *Just alike,* I thought. *They speak and others listen.*

As I ate the rice and drank the tea, Sister told the woman and her sons some of my story. When Sister finished, the old woman shook her head and said, "Very, very sad." She grabbed one of my hands and squeezed it. "No one will be cruel to you here." She looked at her sons and said, "We will be kind to him, won't we, boys?"

Both sons nodded. Even though the men were old enough to have gray in their braids, the old woman called them her little boys. Pointing to one of them, she said, "You may call him Poppa."

I nodded.

"And call him Uncle," she said, pointing to the other son.

I picked up the last grain of rice with my chopsticks and popped it into my mouth. Then I put my head back and tipped the cup completely upside down to get the last drop of the toasty tea. I felt very good. "What shall I call you?" I asked.

"Grandma," she said with a giant smile. "Call me Grandma."

Soon Sister's baby began to cry and the little girls grew tired of petting the lamb. Sister gave a little bow and was gone.

Singing while she worked, Grandma heated some water and washed the dishes. Then she poured the dishwater into a tub and added some hot water. "Come here," she said. "Wash your face and feet. We never go to bed with dirty faces."

I tried not to look at the dirt floor of the hut as I crossed to the tub. Obediently, I washed my face and feet. Afterward, Grandma crouched down, and with tiny, trembling hands she dried first my face and then my feet. "There," she said. "You have washed off the cares of the day. You will sleep clean. Tomorrow you will wake up fresh."

Poppa poked a few pieces of wood into the stove so that the hut would stay warm all night. The brothers removed their shoes and washed their faces and feet. Then Grandma washed and dried herself. When everyone was clean, she pointed to the big straw bed. "You have your own quilt," said Grandma. "What a fine quilt it is, too. Very good."

"My mother made the quilt," I told her.

After the brothers went to bed, Grandma squeezed my hand again. "Go to sleep," she said, pointing to her sons' bed.

So I curled up at the foot of the big straw bed. Grandma crossed the room to cover me with my quilt. Tucking it in around me like a cocoon, she whispered, "Sweet dreams."

Later, from her own bed, she called out to me. "Go to sleep, Chi Fa. Soon it will be morning. Tomorrow I will teach you how to weed the garden. Sweet dreams," she said again.

"Good night, Grandma. Good night, Uncle. Good night, Poppa," I called into the warm, dark room. "Thank you very much."

"I like your quilt. All the way from heaven, your mother reaches long arms and wraps you in love," Grandma whispered. "Very good."

Soon all three were sleeping. I lay awake, listening for a cricket's song, but the snoring was all I could hear. I didn't mind, though. It was a happy tune. Grandma snored through her nose like tiny little pig snorts. One son snored with bursts of air over his teeth. It sounded like the whistle of a boiling pot of water with a dancing lid. The third snores I heard were loud and long with hardly any silence between, like the tooting of a great horn. Though they each played a different snoring instrument, their snores blended in perfect harmony to sing the same peaceful, reassuring song. I knew that I was safe—

safer than I had been since Papa and Mama had died.

Grandma was right about Mama's quilt: I could feel loving arms wrapped around me. And Sister was right: Chi Fa was lucky. There I was in a big straw bed, under Mother's quilt, in a hut, with three strangers who promised never to be cruel to me. The room was warm, and my belly was full. Good fortune had found me.

6
Sky Full
of Dragons
(Be Careful)

當　心

Sometime in the night I kicked off my quilt. It was a wonderful thing to be warm all night. When I got up, Grandma and her sons were sitting at the big table, drinking tea. Grandma asked, "Chi Fa, did you sleep well?"

"Very, very well, thank you, Grandma," I said. "Good morning, Uncle. Good morning, Poppa."

The brothers nodded. Poppa and Uncle never talked to me, though. Sometimes they told Grandma to tell me things. "Tell Chi Fa Poppa wants more tea." Or, "Tell Chi Fa Uncle wants him to get more wood for the fire."

Grandma said they liked me, that I was their

baby. Because her sons had never married, I was the
grandson she had always wanted.

That first morning, she taught me how to weed
the yard. Since there were no rows, it was hard to
tell the vegetables and herb sprouts from the weeds.
When the sun was straight overhead, she said, "Chi
Fa, you may play with the lamb while I make the
tea. Her name is Spring Flower."

The lamb was soft. I liked to pet her. Sometimes
I would take her for a walk, using a rope for a
leash. But never did we let her run loose, because
Grandma said, "If Spring Flower gets the chance,
she will eat the whole garden for one supper."

When the tea was ready, Grandma called, "Chi
Fa-aaaa. Teeee."

Handing me a chipped cup with faded blue flowers painted around the rim, Grandma said, "This
will be your special cup, Chi Fa. I have had it for
many years. My father gave me this cup when I was
a little girl. It was a fine cup then, shiny and new."

"Thank you very much, Grandma," I said.

I liked the cup with blue flowers. It was very old
and beautiful, like Grandma. She filled it with the
delicious lima-bean-shell tea and set a plate of
small, sweet rice cakes on the table. It wasn't the
Celebration of the Moon or any other holiday, and
yet there were sweets with our tea. "Eat as many as
you like," said Grandma.

We laughed as we ate the cakes and drank the
tea. I didn't know a boy could be so happy.

After that first day at Grandma's, every morning when the neighbors' rooster crowed, I would get up and slip out of the hut. I would carry in the wood, build up the fire, boil water, and make tea for Grandma and the brothers. I would take the tea to Grandma in bed. She always said, "Thank you for the tea. You're such a good boy, Chi Fa."

After she drank her morning tea, Grandma would get up and boil rice porridge or make big round wheat cakes. The brothers would eat a big breakfast before going to work in the fields. "See how big my little boys are growing?" Grandma would ask with pride each day when the men left for work.

I didn't eat as fast as Grandma and her sons. I had the habit of chewing my food very slowly so that I could make every mouthful last. Long ago I had learned that if I drank hot tea with rice porridge or wheat cakes, my belly would feel full for most of the day. After the sons left, Grandma would clank around doing the dishes while I finished my breakfast. She'd say, "Chi Fa, we have work to do. Why do you sit there chewing so long?"

"It tastes good, Grandma," I would say. I never left a grain of rice in my bowl, a crumb of wheat cake on my plate, or a drop of tea in my cup. "I like your cooking," I would tell her.

"Very good," Grandma would say.

Grandma and I worked every day in her yard. Although the garden looked like a weed patch, out of the chaos Grandma plucked simple healing. She knew how to grow and pick and dry herbs that could make people well. Grandma was almost blind, so she would tell me, "Chi Fa, bring me some leaves from the plant with the purple flowers." Then she would break a leaf and sniff it. "No, Chi Fa, not the *big* purple flowers. These are morning glories. Bring me leaves from the *little* purple flowers—the wild garlic."

I brought her the things she needed, and she crumbled the flowers, crushed the seeds, and ground the bitter roots. With trembling fingers, she mixed things together and put tiny pinches of herbs in rice paper and folded each into a little packet. "For every ailment on the earth, there is a healing herb," Grandma told me. "The difference between you and me is that I know which herb heals which ailments. It comes from being very ancient," Grandma would say, smiling with her whole sweet face.

I liked being with Grandma. Over and over she asked me to tell my stories. She liked best to hear about my dragon dreams. Sometimes when our work was done, we would lie back in the tall grass on the bank and gaze up into the sky. Grandma couldn't see faraway things like clouds, so she would ask, "Is the sky full of dragons today?"

When I spotted a cloud that looked like it had a head and tail, I would describe how big it was, how round or flat.

"Are the wings long and flapping or short and flittering?" she would want to know. "How fast is it running across the sky? Is it chasing something, Chi

Fa? Tell me everything you see." Although Grandma was nearly blind, she taught me to see skies full of dragons.

Grandma said that when she was a little girl she always dreamed about flying on the back of a big, white swan. So whenever I found a bird's feather in the yard, especially a white one, we would take it inside and wash it and dry it and press it flat. Grandma used the feathers in little bouquets like flowers.

Grandma and I spent a lot of time talking about our dreams. "It is good to have dreams," Grandma told me. "Dreams can carry you anywhere you want to go. Remember that, Chi Fa. Follow your dreams, and go where your heart leads you."

I loved Grandma. So did everyone else. Often women from the village would come to get herbs to heal a sick child or husband. Sometimes people came from far away for this kind of powder or that kind of leaf to make healing teas. "That is how I got Spring Flower," she said. "Last summer, when a traveler came up the canal road with a sick wife and two baby lambs, he left with a well wife and only one lamb," laughed Grandma.

Sometimes she would trade a rice-paper package of healing for a chicken, a handful of rice, or several duck eggs. But never did Grandma take coins for her herbs. "No one owns healing," Grandma would say. "Healing is a gift from heaven."

In the autumn, Grandma's sons hired some field workers to pull the wheat. Since I knew how to use

the dry straw and bamboo to cook, just as I had
done for Communist Mother and Father, I boiled
hot water in the wok, made tea, and delivered the
tea to the workers. I was glad that I could help
Grandma and her sons.

The brothers were happy because they were harvesting a lot of wheat that year. On the last day of
the harvest, Grandma planned a big supper for the
field workers. Before they went to work, Poppa and
Uncle moved the big table outside under a tree. All
day Grandma and I pulled vegetables from her garden—big purple onions, squash, eggplants, and baby
bok choy. Grandma thumped a plump watermelon
that I had been watching grow all summer and said it
was ripe. So the watermelon would get cold, Grandma
instructed me, "Carry the melon to the canal and put
it deep in the water where the current won't steal it."

That was an important job, and I didn't want to
disappoint Grandma. Carefully I carried the big
melon to the canal. I walked along the edge of the
water until I found a tree with big roots growing in
the water. I dug a deep hole in the mud and lodged
the melon in the roots so that it wouldn't float away.

Next Grandma told me to go inside and build a
fire in the stove so that we could cook the vegetables. Later, when Grandma was peeling and slicing
cucumbers, Sister came. "I need healing herbs for
my baby," Sister told Grandma. "Her ears are red,
and she cried all night."

Because of our father's accidental death from the
wrong medicine, Sister didn't trust anyone's healing

herbs except Grandma's. And since Chi Haw was deaf, Sister especially worried when one of her little girls had an earache. I could tell by the look on her face that Sister was worried.

Grandma came into the kitchen and took a little packet from the shelf. "Make some tea for Sister," she said. Then she hurried back outside. "Drop this into some boiling water, and let your baby breathe the steam that rises from the pot," she told her.

My mouth was watering just thinking about the noodle soup, garden vegetables, pan-fried pork, and juicy watermelon. As I fed the fire, I must have put in too much straw, because suddenly I smelled smoke. When I looked up, the flue and part of the straw roof were on fire.

Grandma and Sister ran in. Grandma scooped rice packets of herbs into a big basket. Sister and I grabbed everything we could from off the beds. Within seconds, the whole straw roof was ablaze. Blinded by smoke, arms full, choking and coughing, we stumbled out of the hut. Grandma said, "Oh dear, dear, dear, I care so much for you. Don't worry, Chi Fa."

Red flames changed the blue sky to smoky gray. Strings of burning straw spun upward, and sparks, like fire raining from black clouds of smoke, fish-tailed to the ground. Sister gave me a silent direction with her hand to run away. So I did. Racing up the canal road, I heard Grandma yelling after me, "Don't run away. This is nothing. You're more important. Chi Fa, stop! I love you."

Grandma could not run after me. Soon I was far away, and I could not hear her calling to me. Over my shoulder, I saw smoke from the burning hut filling the sky. I didn't know what to do, so I just ran and ran and ran. After a while I threw myself down on a bank and sobbed. After I'd cried enough tears to fill a bucket, I opened my eyes. The whole sky was gray with smoke. The smell of smoke clung to my clothes. I could even taste the smoke. *Poppa and Uncle must know about the fire by now. They are probably furious,* I told myself.

I just lay there and cried some more. I couldn't believe what had happened. I liked Grandma so much. I liked living in her hut. Now it was burned to the ground.

Within the hour, Sister found me. "Lucky for you that I was there, Chi Fa," said Sister, handing me Mama's quilt.

Lucky? How can Sister think I am lucky today? I asked myself. "Oh, Sister, whatever will I do? I burned down Grandma's hut."

"Grandma is okay. I waited with her until her sons came running. She knows it was an accident, but her sons are fuming," said Sister. "It was a tragic thing. We cannot know what her sons will do next. You cannot go back there right now, and you cannot hide at my house, either. That is the first place the brothers will come looking for you. I must find you a place to hide until this whole thing is forgotten."

"But I want to be with Grandma," I begged Sister. "The special supper was to be tonight."

"Sorry, Chi Fa, there will be no supper tonight. You cannot be with Grandma. Now, come along."

With hurried steps, Sister glided along the road ahead of me. This time I heard no words of advice. Instead, loud silence filled the air. I wished Sister would tell me I was a good boy, or even tell me I was a bad boy. I wished she would give me advice. But nothing. Only silence. My heart was heavy.

I am a good boy, but I caused a terrible accident. I should have been more careful, I thought. "Next time I will be more careful," I told Sister.

"If people ask a boy to do a man's work, they cannot complain when there is trouble. It is not your fault, Chi Fa. You were doing your best," said Sister. "Now, hurry along. I have a sick baby at home."

As we rushed along the road toward Sister's house, she stopped at each door, trying to find someone who would take me in for the night. "So sorry," they all said, "there is no room here for a boy."

After a dozen people had shut their doors in our faces, Sister asked, "Oh, Chi Fa, what will we do? I cannot take you home. Chi Haw will have learned about the fire by now. I know you have been through a lot today, but my own baby is sick."

Sister sat down on a big, flat rock and put her face in her hands and wept. I didn't know if she was crying for me or for Grandma or for her sick baby. Maybe she was crying for herself. Sister was good and deserved more happiness than she had.

"Don't cry, Sister," I said, squeezing her hand the way Grandma had squeezed mine. "Everything will be okay. I have my quilt. I can sleep here tonight. Go home to your baby. Tomorrow things will be better. Please, go home." I knew Sister didn't want to leave me, but her sigh told me she had no choice. I said, "See this big tree? I will sleep here tonight. I will stay right here until you come for me tomorrow."

"You are very brave," Sister sobbed, wiping away tears. "Sometimes the easy way seems the hardest." She stood, and without another word, Sister was gone.

I lay down on the ground under the quilt. I curled up in a tight little ball and tucked one arm under my head. The ground was cold and hard. I tossed and turned. I thought about the watermelon, deep in the hole in the mud, lodged in the roots. Too sad to sleep, I got up and gathered armloads of fallen leaves and busied myself making a soft bed. Then I curled up on the leaf bed, under the quilt again, and tried to rest. I told myself, *Grandma dried my feet. She gave me lima-bean-shell tea and sweet rice cakes, even when it wasn't a holiday. At Grandma's was the very first time I got to play. I loved Grandma, and she loved me. Now we can't be together.*

Even the moon looked sad. Never could I remember feeling so miserable. Hungry and heartsick, I cried myself to sleep.

7
The
Stranger's
House
(Be Kind)

仁 慈

It was a long, restless night. At dawn someone gently kicked me. Jumping to my feet, I found myself staring into the wild eyes of a short, unkempt man. His long hair, like unbundled hay, stuck out every which way. I was too surprised to speak. He placed a small rice cake in my hand, and, silent as a slug, he slipped away and disappeared in the morning mist.

When I had time to realize I was awake and not dreaming, I called out, "Thank you for the cake."

It was very cold, so I sat down, wrapped Mama's quilt around my shoulders, and very slowly ate the cake. Off in the distance, a rooster crowed. Billowy clouds, like huge puffs of smoke, hung on the horizon.

The rising sun, an emerging, fire-breathing dragon, set the sky ablaze.

"If there hadn't been a fire yesterday, right now, I would be petting Spring Flower and gathering wood," I thought. I wondered where Grandma slept last night. I worried that she was sad and that her sons were angry. I worried about Sister. I wondered if the baby was okay. I just sat there and worried. Then I worried some more. I didn't know one boy could have so much worry inside of him.

Before long, with baby in arms and three little girls trailing, Sister came. "Baby is well. See? She is happy."

"She looks happy," I told Sister.

I looked at each of my nieces. They giggled. The sound of their happiness made me feel better.

"I have some good news," said Sister. "I found a place where you may hide. Come along before someone sees you."

Gliding along the road ahead of me, Sister said, "The man you will be staying with is sometimes sick." Then she stopped and faced me. Wagging a finger, she said, "Be patient. You can help him, Chi Fa. Remember to be kind."

"I will remember," I promised Sister, folding my quilt into a bundle as we went.

"You are lucky, Chi Fa. I didn't think that I could find you a place, but the first door that I went to this morning was opened to you." When Sister stopped, we were standing in front of a house only a block from where she lived.

"Who lives here?" I asked her.

"This is the house of only one man. Since his mother died last winter, he lives alone," said Sister. "His mother used to take care of him. Now you will take care of him."

"How can I take care of a grown-up?" I asked.

"Chi Fa, you can build his fires and clean his house."

"Sister," I said, "I cannot build a fire. I am afraid."

"You must, Chi Fa," said Sister. "The man's affliction makes it impossible for him to care for himself. Sometimes he will do strange things. But just remember, it is his sickness that causes him to act in odd ways. Be kind. Do not be afraid. The man is your only hope, and you are his."

Sister knocked.

"What strange things does he do, Sister?"

As Sister opened her mouth to speak, the door swung open. Much to my surprise, there stood the same disheveled man who had given me the rice cake at dawn. He motioned with his arm for us to come inside.

Sister's baby cried at the sight of him. I, too, felt like crying, but I was not a baby. "We must go," said Sister, and off they went.

I wanted to run away too, but I had nowhere to go except inside. I squared my shoulders and followed the man into the big room. It was cold and dark inside. Soon my eyes adjusted to the dim light, and I could see charred walls and a dirty floor. There was a table with two chairs, a stove, and a big, fancy wood-framed bed with mosquito netting all around it. The broom, bucket, and tub in one corner looked as though they had not been used for quite some time. There was no wood piled near the stove. The shelves were empty—not a bite to eat in the house. I was grateful for a place to sleep, but the odor in the room made me want to rush outside for fresh air. Remembering Sister's words, I told myself, *"Be kind."*

I laid my quilt on the bed. The man didn't say a word to me at all that day. He just sat in his chair, staring out the window. In fact, in the months to come, we never had a conversation. I spent the first day cleaning the room. I drew water from his well and went outside to get sticks to build a fire. Nothing grew in the man's yard except one tree, so I walked along the canal bank and gathered an armload of dried bamboo sticks to build a fire.

Back inside the kitchen, I poured water into a large pan and very carefully built a small fire. When the water was warm, I removed the two thin, tattered blankets from his bed and washed them in the tub of hot water and then hung them up to dry on a low branch of the big tree in his yard. I shook the dust from the mosquito netting around the bed. I swept the floor, and scrubbed the table and floor as best I could. The floor was spotted with something dark that looked like bloodstains. After I finished cleaning the room, I heated more water and washed my face and feet. I asked the man if he wanted to wash, but he didn't answer.

By nightfall I was very hungry. I had eaten nothing except the stale rice cake before dawn. There wasn't a bit of food in the house—no rice or flour. I went outside and brought in the blankets and made the bed. Carefully, I spread my quilt on top of the thin blankets. When the sun, like a snail, crept away for the day, leaving but a cold, dark trail of black clouds, I crawled under the clean blankets and quilt. The bed and room smelled fresh and clean now. "Good night," I called from the bed.

Still sitting in his chair by the window, with the light of the half-moon shining on his face, the man looked like a ghost. I was afraid to go to sleep. I waited and waited for him to come to bed. After what seemed like half the night, I heard him snoring in his chair at the window. I closed my eyes and slept too. During that fitful night, each time his snoring stopped, the silence woke me. The whole night through was like that—listening, sleeping, listening, sleeping. Before dawn, he rose from his chair and went out. Feeling safe, I fell into a deep sleep.

In the brightness of the morning's light, I awoke to find that he was back sitting in his chair. "Good morning," I greeted him, crawling out from under the warm covers and stretching.

I took a morning walk along the canal again, gathering sticks as I went. Soon my arms were full of dried bamboo branches, and I went back inside to build another little fire. I heated some water. There was no tea, so I drank a cup of steaming water. I used the rest of the water to wash my face and the glass panes in the windows.

At noon, Sister knocked on the door with a little tin box that held rice and vegetables and two shrimp—the same foods that she had brought to me at the canal over a year before. I offered to share my meal with the man, but he didn't seem to hear me.

While I ate, Sister gave me good news. "Grandma, Uncle, and Poppa are fine. They are staying with one of their neighbors. The sons are going to rebuild the hut. They have plenty of hay left from the harvest for a new roof," she said with a reassuring smile.

I was lonely for Grandma but relieved that things could be fixed. As soon as I finished eating, I asked, "Sister, may we go for a walk?"

Outside, where the man could not hear me, I asked her, "What is wrong with him? He doesn't speak. He doesn't eat. He sleeps sitting up in his chair."

"Chi Fa, he is your only hope," she said.

"Sister," I said, "I am afraid of him."

"He will not hurt you. Just be kind."

"What is wrong with the man?" I asked again.

"He has seizures sometimes," said Sister, "but he will not harm you. I will bring you food each time Chi Haw goes out. I cannot promise I will come every day, but I will try. You must stay here. Don't make a fuss."

Sister had spoken. There was nothing left to be said. I was to stay at the house with the man.

Each day was the same. Before dawn, he would

go out and then come home, and sit in his chair, staring out the window. In all those months, I saw him eat only once. Soon I figured out that when he left each morning before dawn, he was going out to beg for his daily meal. That's what he had been doing when I saw him that first morning. I often thought about the first night in the man's house when I went to bed hungry, because I had only eaten one stale rice cake at dawn. Later I realized that the man had been twice as hungry as I that night, because that morning he had given me his only food for the day.

One bleak morning a wintry wind shook the windowpanes, and something terrible happened. The man stood up, stiffened like a board, and collapsed into the table, knocking the clay water pot to the floor, where it shattered. With eyes rolled back in his head, he jerked and writhed amidst the sharp fragments, screaming horrible things—words I did not understand.

Alarmed that he would cut himself upon the jagged pieces, I dropped across his body and grabbed his arms. But with a bull's strength, he mindlessly flung me headfirst into the wall. The blow left me frightened and dazed, but I didn't forget my responsibility for his safety. Dodging his thrashing arms and legs, I kicked the sharp pieces away from him against the wall. But even with this threat removed, he hurt himself. He bit his tongue, and bloody foam frothed from his lips.

I was so afraid. Shaking, I ran outside and waited until the screaming stopped. When I had gathered my courage, I went back inside and found him lying asleep on the floor with his face in a pool of vomit.

That seizure was the scariest thing that I had ever seen, but after witnessing several more fits, I grew less afraid. Eventually I attempted to help him during his seizures by sitting near him and speaking calmly. "You are a good man," I would say. "You will be better soon." Over and over I repeated, "You are a good man."

After each convulsion stopped, I soothed his head with a cool rag and washed his face. I rubbed his chest and held his hand. For a long time afterward, he'd just lie, exhausted, on the floor. When he woke up, I would help him into his chair and then scrub the floor.

Only after he knew that I had grown comfortable with his affliction did the man begin to sleep in the bed with me at night. In the beginning, he had known that I was afraid of him and had slept sitting up all those nights because he was kind. I gradually realized that my friend was gentle and tender-hearted. In his frailty he taught me strength.

Sister brought food whenever Chi Haw was not at home. She usually came once a day. Once in a while she came twice a day. Sometimes, unfortunately, Chi Haw did not go away, and she couldn't come for several days. On such occasions, I went hungry. As frequently as she could, Sister surprised us with candles, tea, or bamboo to burn in the stove.

Most days during that autumn and winter, I took walks along the canal bank, picking up dried sticks so that we could have fires. Twice a day I lit the stove long enough to heat water for making tea and washing. My friend enjoyed the tea very much. Before going to bed each night, I poured warm water in a tub and washed my face and feet. Afterward, I washed his face and feet and dried them, like Grandma had taught me. Once a week I washed, brushed, and braided his hair.

In October 1949, when the People's Republic of China was formally established and Beijing was named the new capital, I was busy taking care of my friend. I didn't know that all of China was in turmoil. Day after day we sat in our chairs, staring out the window at the big tree with bare branches pointing at odd angles toward the sky. Side by side, we watched as the world turned brown. The sun seldom showed its face, and when it did, the hazy light had no warmth. Through the window, it coldly illuminated the white vapor of our breath.

Sticks and bamboo fuel were scarce, so I could build only short-lived fires to boil water for tea. The winter months were bitter cold inside my friend's house. I would wrap a blanket around his shoulders, and then wrap Mama's quilt around me. Unaware of the changing world around us, we were cocooned like two caterpillars waiting for spring. On New Year's Day, Sister brought us rice balls with black sesame seeds inside. I talked my friend into eating one for good luck.

Finally, one bright day, the sun began to shine and warm the earth again. It was the spring of 1950, the year of the tiger. I was nine and a half years old.

Tiny green sprouts were popping up everywhere. Soon the big tree in the man's yard was perfumed with peach blossoms. Often I spoke of how the ripe peaches would taste. I promised to pick every single one for him. But while the peaches were still green, no bigger than walnuts, Sister came with news that would change my life again.

Smiling, she handed me a bundle of clothes and some lunch. While I ate the bowl of vegetables, Sister said, "I have good news, Chi Fa. I have saved enough rice to buy you a barge ticket to Shanghai, where you will live with Ching Fa. I will come for you at dawn. Wash your hair and put on the clean clothes."

The news so surprised me that it was hard to swallow my lunch. Afterward, when I curiously unfolded the clothes, what I saw practically made my heart stop. "Sister, I do not mean to be disrespectful; I am glad to go to Shanghai," I said. "But these are women's clothes. I cannot walk in women's bonded shoes."

Sister shook her finger at me, and with her crossest voice she said, "Chi Fa, I do not have men's clothes that I can give you. These clothes and old bonded shoes are the only shoes I could get for you. I have been hiding a little rice each day for months to get enough to buy your barge ticket. Do not complain. Be ready at dawn." Then Sister rushed away.

I stood there looking at the clothes. I knew I could not wear what I was wearing. The pants were two inches too short and threadbare. I had been wearing the same clothes all winter and half the spring. I didn't own a pair of shoes. I'd outgrown mine many months before. If I was going to Shanghai, I had to obey Sister.

"Look at these clothes that I have to wear to Shanghai," I told my friend.

He did not turn his head to look. He just stared out the window at two butterflies that had landed on the windowsill. I went to him, and together we watched the butterflies fluttering their colorful wings in the warm spring sunlight. They stayed there, side by side, for a short spell. Then one flew off, while the other one watched it go. For months I had wondered if my friend understood anything that happened around him; when I saw a tear roll down his face, I knew he had understood everything.

I heated water and made us the last tea that we would ever share. With the remaining warm water, I bathed both of us and washed our hair. As I brushed and braided, I talked to him. "I will miss you," I told him. "Remember, you are a good man. You have been a friend to me. I will never forget you." I squeezed his hand and went to bed. "I care for you," I called to him. "Good night."

He didn't come to bed. He slept sitting up in his chair at the window.

The next morning when I got up to get ready to leave, my friend had already gone begging for his daily meal. I put on the women's clothes and shoes. I felt foolish. The bonded shoes were too small and hurt my feet. I folded up Mama's quilt and tucked it under my arm. I looked around the room one last time. My friend had never talked to me or squeezed my hand the way Grandma had, but I knew that he cared for me. We were friends. We were alike—both orphans. Without words, he had taught me many things. I asked myself, *What will he do without me? Who will make him tea? He cannot safely build fires. Who will wash his face and braid his hair? Who will rub his head and hold his hand after his seizures?*

Quickly I unrolled Mama's quilt and carefully spread it back out on his bed. Then I slipped out into the early light to wait for Sister.

PART II

SHANGHAI

1950–1951

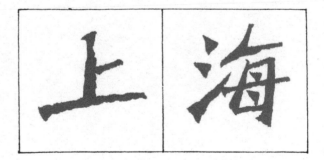

8

On the Barge

(Be Sympathetic)

憐 憫

The sky was blue and clear. I heard her before I saw her. Sister was pushing my cart with two one-hundred-pound bags of rice—the price of a barge ticket for one boy to go to Shanghai. "We must hurry," Sister said.

I took the cart handles and followed her.

As she hurried along the road ahead of me, she said, "Brother will be there to meet you when you arrive in Shanghai. You may find Brother is very bitter. He is working as a shoeshine man. Pride makes it hard for him to serve others. He can no longer pretend to be wealthy. Sister-in-Law is working as a maid for a rich family, and that makes Brother even more resentful."

I did not know what to say about Brother's pain. My own pain, the suffering of walking in very small shoes, brought stinging tears to my eyes. Still, I tried to concentrate on what Sister was telling me.

"Shanghai is a gigantic city, Chi Fa, larger than you can even imagine. A small boy can be swallowed up by a place that big." Then, stopping in her tracks and turning to face me, she wagged a finger. "Promise me you won't get into trouble in Shanghai," she commanded.

"I promise," I told Sister. Then I sat down on the side of the canal road and tore off the shoes and put them in the cart. Already, big red blisters covered my feet.

As luck would have it, we had to walk by Grandma's new hut. It looked the same, except the roof was new, bright yellow straw. Spring Flower, much bigger now, was tethered in the blossom-filled yard. Smoke curled from the chimney. I knew how it sounded inside the hut—snoring in perfect harmony. I wanted to rush inside and make Grandma a cup of tea and take it to her in bed. I wanted to hear her say, "Thank you for the tea. You're such a good boy, Chi Fa."

"Hurry along. If you stop, you will miss the barge," scolded Sister.

"May I just pet Spring Flower?" I asked.

"No time for petting the lamb. Come along."

With each step away from my village, I began to worry. I was going far away to a big city—a place that could swallow up a small boy. Would I ever

again see Favorite Uncle? Or Sister and her little
girls? I was certain I would never again see Grandma
or my new friend. Tears gushed from my eyes. I
said, "Please tell Grandma how much I miss her.
And will you sometimes stop and make tea for my
friend? He likes tea, and he can't build a fire to heat
water."

With a wave of her hand, Sister promised to look
in on them both.

"Sister," I said, "I will miss you and your little
girls."

"Do not worry, Chi Fa. I will see you soon. The
Communist government is taking nearly all of Chi
Haw's many fields. He is angry and plans to leave
here. Soon we will join you in Shanghai, and we
hope to escape to Hong Kong, too."

I was too young to understand about Communism. The only thing I understood was that soon I
would see Sister again. "I am happy you will come
to Shanghai. I will wait to see you," I told her.

When we finally reached the barge, Sister told
me to put on the shoes, and she went back to give
the captain of the barge the rice.

When she came back, she said, "Remember, Chi
Fa, you are lucky. Good fortune will find you." Then
Sister took hold of the handles of the empty cart and
started back.

"Sister," I said, struggling in the bonded shoes to
catch up with her, "I will think of you." I hugged her
a long good-bye.

Every step in the tight shoes brought tears to my

eyes. Hoping no one would notice me in the women's clothes, I sat and only nodded when people looked at me. My thinking was this: *If everyone thinks I am a woman, they will not tease me about my clothes and shoes.*

The problem was, the captain of the barge knew I was a boy. By the day's end, he was itching to let everyone know my secret. "Attention! I must count all the people on the barge," he shouted. "First, I need all the women to raise their hands."

I did not raise my hand. A few people looked at me, and then a few more. Pretty soon every eye on the barge was glaring at me.

Walking up to me, the captain said, "Woman, why didn't you raise your hand to be counted?"

My voice would tell everyone that I was a boy, so I did not speak.

"Why are you not raising your hand?" he asked again.

My face was red, and I was burning with embarrassment, but still I did not speak.

"Maybe you are not a woman. Maybe you are a boy just pretending to be a woman," he announced loudly.

"Oh!" gasped several women in the crowd.

"Shall we find out? What if I look under your skirt?" the captain said, grabbing at me.

"I am a boy!" I shouted. "These are Sister's clothes," I tried to explain, but the laughter drowned out my small voice.

"It's a little boy," someone snickered.

"Look at that ridiculous boy in women's clothes," said a very fat woman.

They did not care about an orphan who was too poor to own a pair of pants and shoes. They did not want to hear about Grandma and how her hut had burned down. No one cared about my friend who went begging each morning for his only meal of the day and sat in a chair staring out the window the rest of the time. Another's pain was not important to them. They only wanted someone to point a finger at and tease.

"Wild boy!" shouted a man.

"Boy who thinks he is a woman," teased another man.

"She's pretty sweet," jeered a third man.

I looked at the three old men. Their pointed noses and little brown teeth jutted out. They looked like rats. To myself I said, *Triplets. Rat triplets.*

I remembered what the very old man had told me the day he gave me the great pile of cakes: "Better to be a young man with an empty belly than an old man with a full belly."

I had to learn to shield myself because, from that moment on, the jeering never stopped. And although day after day, for ten days, I had to endure sharp barbs, I had yet another, more serious, problem— getting enough to eat. When the captain cooked the rice for the passengers, just before the rice was done, he poured off the extra water. He called it soup. "Here, have some soup, little girl," he would say, handing me a bowl of rice water.

Then he'd finish cooking the rice until it was tender for the passengers who had paid coins, instead
of rice, to ride the barge. Day after day it was like
that. I was skin and bones, sick and miserable. The
bonded shoes hurt my feet, and I could barely walk.
To make things even worse, on the third day, I discovered my head was covered with lice.

There was nothing to do on the barge. There
wasn't room for the passengers to walk about or
cook or do work. For fun they had only a little boy
dressed in women's clothes to torment. Everyone
aboard teased me, especially the very fat woman
and the rat triplets. The very fat woman never grew
tired of saying vicious things to me. "You are disgusting in those clothes." Or, "Why do you pretend
to be a woman? Are you crazy?"

Always one of the rat triplets would chime in,
"Isn't she sweet?" Every time people forgot to tease
me, the very fat woman would remind them again.
The only time she wasn't using her tongue to say
cruel things was when she was eating. She talked to
me just like I was a dog—worse than a dog!

One afternoon I begged the captain for a cup of
water, but he said, "Go away, little girl. Can't you see
I am busy?"

I was very thirsty, and finally I decided to try to
get a little water from the river. I went to the front of
the barge and leaned over the edge of one side. I
was scooping up the water with my hands when I
lost my balance and fell into the cold river. I could
not swim. I held my breath and grabbed the side of

the barge. I realized the only thing I could do was stay afloat. The barge pulled me along for quite some time. My arms grew tired of holding on, but I knew that if the barge got away from me, even if I could manage to get to shore, I would be lost in a strange place without food. I would die.

All the people on the barge were watching and laughing, but nobody offered a hand to help me. Finally, I pulled myself up out of the water and crawled back onto the barge. I heard the very fat woman yell, "He needed a bath anyway! He stinks."

All together it took ten days to reach Shanghai Harbor. Those were long, hot, painful, humiliating days. As the barge came in to shore, I tried to spot Brother waiting in the crowd of people on the dock.

An important thing I forgot to mention is China's class system. At that time, in China, if a person was from the north, or if he was a field worker, or if he was this or that, people would look down on him. People from the north were often called pigs.

So there we were, a bargeload of pigs from the north, landing in Shanghai. As we got off the barge, we had to walk down a pier that was crowded with people on either side. At the far end of the dock, I spotted Brother. I waved and waved, but he didn't wave back.

"Look at the northern pigs. Oink, Oink!" shouted a man on the dock.

"Give that hog plenty of room," yelled another man.

"Here's some slop for the sow," said a man, kicking muddy water on the very fat woman.

"Watch her waddle," chided a man with a big scar on his face.

Everyone laughed loudly, but for the first time in a long time, the teasing was not directed at me. The people were mostly shouting at the very fat woman.

"Look at that ridiculous fat woman," laughed a woman wearing a hat with a peacock's feather sticking up high.

I was right behind the very fat woman, and I could hear her gasping for air. She huffed and puffed as she shuffled her tiny feet along. Suddenly misfortune found her. She stumbled. She fell. Dazed, she lay facedown on the ground. When she started struggling to get to her feet, I backed up to give her room. The crowd was loud, like at the end of a dog fight. They barked and howled. "Get up, Piggy. Get up!" someone yelped.

She was too heavy to get up. After a fitful struggle, rolling over was all she could manage. The very fat woman sat up and said many bad words. I felt very sorry for her. I knew how it felt to be laughed at. I walked around her and grabbed both of her hands. I pulled with all my might to help her stand, but she was too heavy for one boy to lift. "Help me, Brother," I called, motioning for him with one arm.

Brother just looked around as if he didn't know me. Finally one of the rat triplets came up and got under one of the very fat woman's arms. He told me to get up under her other arm. So I did. She was hot and sweaty. "On three," he said, "lift." Then he counted, "One. Two. Three. Lift."

I lifted, but the very fat woman didn't budge off the ground even an inch. Everyone laughed. "Again," he said. "One. Two. Three. Lift." This time she came up some but fell back down with a big thud. The very fat woman said some more bad words.

The man under her arm motioned for the other rat triplets to go around behind her. When they were in place, he told them to get ready to push. This time the crowd counted, "One. Two. Three. Lift!"

I pushed up with all my might. The woman stood up so quickly she almost toppled over frontwards. Back and forth she rocked on her tiny feet. I held my breath. The rocking slowed. She steadied herself, then stood there with a wild look on her face, her hair sticking up every which way. In the back, her skirt was hiked up, and everyone behind her could see her huge upper thighs.

"Ham hocks!" yelled the man with the scar. "Northern ham hocks."

Quickly I pulled the very fat woman's skirt down and brushed her off.

"Don't touch me," she said, swatting at me as though I were a gnat. Then with her nose held high in the air, the very fat woman waddled away.

9
Brother's Place

(Be Forgiving)

I ran up to Brother and tried to shake his hand. "Stay away," he snapped, jumping back, "you're covered with lice."

Clearly, Brother was not happy to see me. Hurriedly he left the dock. "Brother," I yelled, trying to keep up while wearing the tight shoes, "how is Nephew?"

He did not answer. He just rushed along the road. People on bicycles, in cars, and in rickshaws rumbled along the narrow, twisting streets.

Suddenly he turned sharply, and we were on a busy street in the biggest city I had ever seen. Sister was right, Shanghai was gigantic! Big wooden skyscrapers with glass windows—such sights I had

never seen! Along the market area, both sides of the
street were lined with places that sold food.

My mouth watered, looking at the fruit and vegetables piled high on wooden carts and the cooked
meat and rice that gave off delicious aromas.

It hurt to run, but I stayed on Brother's heels. If I
got lost, I knew I would never find my way. I was
dizzy from hunger. I hadn't eaten anything except
rice water for over a week. The street was crowded. I
could not see over or around people, so I just ran
down a path that Brother divided through the
crowd. It was very noisy. I couldn't even hear my
own thoughts.

After walking for what seemed like a very long
time, Brother made another turn onto a little street.
From the back alleyway we entered and climbed
stairs to a small room. Inside, Nephew and a man
and a woman sat on wooden benches at a table.
Nephew smiled at me. The woman at the table was
not Sister-in-Law. At least I didn't think a woman
could change so much in four years. In the dim light
of the room, I studied the woman's heavy red eyelids
and toothless face. I tried to remember what Sister-
in-Law looked like. In the end, I could not decide if
it was she or not. I just stood there in women's
clothes and bonded shoes, waiting for someone to
say something to me. Finally Brother said, "This
is my little sister, Chi Fa." The man and woman
laughed.

Brother gave me a small bowl of vegetables and

rice. Nephew gave me the chopsticks. I thanked them with a nod. As soon as I finished my meal, Brother told Nephew to get me some clothes and show me where to bathe. Nephew pulled some things from a stack of his clothes in one corner of the room and told me to follow him. Back down the stairs I went. We took a path about a quarter mile to a canal. A few sampans floated on the water. "This is where we get our water," said Nephew. "This is where we take baths and wash our clothes."

I sat down and took off the bonded shoes. I placed them side by side on the ground. I saw Nephew looking at the festering blisters on my feet. He picked up one of the women's shoes and tossed it into the canal. As the little shoe bobbed on top of the water and then floated out of sight, a great relief washed over me. Laughter bellowed from my chest.

With a grin, Nephew picked up the other shoe and handed it to me. Without hesitation, I threw it as hard as I could. It made a big splash when it landed in the water. I laughed as it bobbed about for a bit before a big branch sticking up out of the water snagged it. The current rushed around it, but the shoe didn't budge. Picking up stones and tossing them at the little shoe, together we began to laugh hard. By the time the shoe was free and floating away, we were both holding our bellies and laughing until tears rolled down our faces. It felt good to see that little shoe disappear down the canal. All the misery of the barge, like the bonded shoes, slowly floated downstream.

Laughed out, I waded into the cold water and washed myself as best I could. I unbraided my long hair and tried to scrub out the lice. Then I stepped out of the canal, shook the water from my body, and went behind a tree. I took off the wet clothes and put on the clothes Nephew had brought for me. When he came around the tree, I looked at him. He looked at me, and each knew what the other was thinking. We began to laugh again. I picked up the pile of women's clothes and walked to the edge of the water, and I threw them as hard as I could. Wet and heavy, the clothes made a splash only a few feet in front of me. Slowly they sank into the muddy water along the edge of the canal. We watched as the current finally grabbed hold of them and pulled them away. Then Nephew and I began laughing all over again. For the first time in days, I felt free and happy. I didn't know what to expect in Shanghai, but I thought, *Nothing can be as bad as wearing women's clothes and bonded shoes.*

It felt wonderful to walk barefoot back to the house. On the way, Nephew told me about the woman and man I had seen with Brother. "That is their house," he said. "Papa pays them for us to live there. We don't see Mama very much. She is a maid in a big, fancy house. She only comes to see us every other Sunday."

I could tell by his face that Nephew missed his mama.

When we climbed the stairs and went back into the room, I felt Brother staring at me. I wondered if he could tell we had been laughing so hard. He did not speak.

I said, "Thank you very much for the clothes and a place to stay, Brother." Coming from the north, I used a different dialect. When the couple heard my words, they snickered. Although they were very, very poor, they were Shanghaians. Like the people on the dock, they looked down on northerners. What followed was the same kind of welcome the dock people had given the very fat woman. Although Brother was from the north too, he didn't seem to hear their cruel remarks.

Just before dark, Brother took me outside in the alley. With a dull pair of scissors, he gave me a haircut. When most of my hair lay on the ground at my feet, he handed me a brown bar of soap and told me to go wash my hair again. So Nephew and I walked back to the canal. This time, I soaped my hair and scrubbed hard; the strong brown soap seared my scalp like fire. Nephew said he could see the lice jumping off my head, trying to get away.

The next morning, at the breakfast table, the woman rubbed her drooping red eyelids and told Brother, "If the boy is staying, I expect extra rent each month."

"Chi Fa will earn his keep," promised Brother.

"Fine," said the woman. "From now on, Chi Fa, you will cook the rice. You will wash the dishes. You will scrub the floors. You will carry the water."

I didn't mind the tasks. Long ago I had learned how to work hard. Many times each day I walked to

the canal with a big jar and filled it with water and
carried the heavy load back to the house and up the
stairs. I purified the water we drank by dissolving a
hard crystal-like cake in each jar. I kept the room
scrubbed and everyone's clothes washed and folded.
Each morning and night, I cooked the rice and
washed the dishes.

I had been in Shanghai nearly two weeks before
Sister-in-Law came for a visit. Brother sent Nephew
and me out so that he could be alone with her. We
walked around the narrow, winding streets peering
into the windows. We stayed out until the sun
dropped from the sky and then hurried home.

By then, Sister-in-Law was eager to get back to
the comfort of the house where she slept in a big
straw bed and ate good food every day. Brother
urged her to stay the night, but she scurried off. That
evening Brother and Nephew pouted and went to
sleep early.

Often in the hot summertime, after I finished
cleaning up and washing the clothes, and before it
was time to cook supper, Nephew and I would go to
the canal to play in the water. Those first few months
things went pretty well; but in the autumn, as the
weather cooled, so did Brother. And as the days
grew shorter, so did Brother's patience. Every day he
became more difficult to please.

By winter, Brother had grown as bitter and cruel
as the nights. I didn't always cook the rice just right.
If the rice was not prepared perfectly, Brother would
hit me. Always when he beat me, I would say to

myself, *Brother is angry because his wife lives in a beautiful house with rich people. He is ashamed because he used to own the village store, but now he shines the shoes of the store owners.*

One dreary winter afternoon, when Brother's mood was as dark as the day, he turned on me. I remember it clearly. I was getting ready to cook supper. Brother looked in the pan where I was washing the rice and said, "This rice looks dirty!"

Before I had time to say I would rewash the rice, he picked up a sharp bamboo stick and began hitting me with it. Yelling, "I will not eat dirty rice!" he chased me around the room, battering me with the bamboo stick.

Each blow stung and cut my skin. Soon welts on my back and arms and legs were bleeding. I stumbled and fell and crawled into a corner. For protection, I put my hands and arms up over my head. But he kept on switching me. "Stop!" I begged.

Brother did not listen. The switch seemed to have a life of its own. Like a cobra with cornered prey, it struck again and again. Fortunately, Brother finally lost his grip and the switch flew out of his hand. I sprang to my feet and ran down the stairs as fast as my throbbing limbs would carry me. I didn't stop, or even look back, until I'd reached the canal. Realizing he was not on my heels, I walked into the water and washed off the blood and tried to clean the deep cuts. Then I dragged myself to shore and, in pain, rested on the cold bank. To soothe myself, I searched the sky for dragon clouds, but there wasn't even one in sight.

Afraid to go home, I sat there shivering for what seemed like hours. When finally the shining moon rose out of the canal and reflected its twin on the water, I saw Brother walking up the canal road toward town. I knew he would stay out late drinking and gambling, so it was safe to go home. I limped back and climbed the stairs. I was curled up in a tight ball on my mat when I heard a voice say, "Here's some rice for you."

Nephew gently touched my arm. I sat up and took the rice. He did not speak again. The bowl of rice was Nephew's way of saying he was sorry for me.

Even my jaws ached, but I finished the rice, and Nephew took the bowl from me. I lay down and closed my eyes.

When morning's first light woke me, pain shot through every inch of me, but the place that hurt the most was my heart. Knowing that Brother hated me was my greatest anguish.

After that incident, Brother never had a kind word for me. Whatever I did, whatever I said, it was always the wrong thing. I swallowed his harsh words and accepted each bitter beating in silence. And after every attack, I tried my best to forgive Brother. My thinking was this: *Brother is not angry with Chi Fa. Brother is angry with his position in life.*

I had another big problem that made me miserable: trying to keep warm at night. There was no protection from the wind and cold that howled through the mud walls. The house stayed damp and chilly all winter. There were no straw beds. I slept on the floor with only one thin, tattered blanket over me.

Each of the others had a thick rubber bag they filled with boiling water and put under their blankets to keep them warm through the night. But I did not have one of those hot-water bags, so my nights were long and bitter cold. That is why I especially remember a Sunday visit Sister-in-Law made in late December 1950, the year of the tiger.

She came with an armload of packages, a big bag of sweet oranges, and a box of nuts in shells. There was also a round tin that held a little cake full of dried fruits and nuts and rum. She told us about some American missionaries who were hiding from the Communists in the big house where she worked. "In America, tonight is Christmas Eve," she said. "There they celebrate the birth of a baby boy named Jesus by giving gifts."

Sister-in-Law gave each of us a present, wrapped in red-and-green tissue paper and tied with a ribbon. Brother got a handsome pair of leather shoes that he said he could polish and make look like new. Nephew unwrapped a nice wooden box with a hinged lid. It was filled with colorful mah-jongg tiles. For the woman there was perfume in a tiny blue bottle. The man got a pair of brown wool socks, with only a very tiny hole in one, which he wore to bed every night that winter. But I got the best gift of all: my own hot-water bag! I thought, *Sister-in-Law is sorry she sold me to the Communist chief. That is why she is giving me such a fine gift.*

Sister-in-Law boiled tea and cut the cake into six pieces. She gave the biggest piece to Nephew. As I sipped the hot tea and ate my slice of sweet cake, I listened to the adults murmuring about the terrible things the Japanese soldiers had done to Chinese people during the war. The man who lived in the house said the Communists had saved China from the Japanese. Brother did not speak of the Communists. I knew that Brother did not like it that the Communists had taken over China, but he did not speak of such things. Now, no one in China spoke openly against the Communists.

Often that winter, warmed by the hot-water bag resting on my chest, I had good dragon dreams. Arms wrapped around my dragon's big, strong neck, I soared above the world, where all my cares seemed smaller than they did in the daytime. And always, when it was time to wake up, first I landed in America.

In 1951, the year of the rabbit, we celebrated the Chinese New Year by watching a long parade of paper dragons weaving through the street. Communist soldiers carrying Chinese Communist flags and posters of Mao Tse-tung led the parade. When it got dark, fireworks filled the sky. Never had I seen such a thing! Firecrackers split the night: *Pop! Pop! Pop!* At that sound, I wanted to run away and hide because it reminded me of Communist Father and that awful night in the community building. If Sister had not rescued me from the Communist parents, I wondered if by now I would be a Communist, too.

In the spring, with budding leaves and blossoms, came important changes: Brother went to Hong Kong. A week later, Sister-in-Law lost her job, because the Communists arrested the American missionaries and the owners of the house who had been hiding them. They were all to be tried as political enemies. Sister-in-Law was afraid she might be arrested, too.

One night, when I sat alone on the canal bank gazing up, the moon's full face seemed to smile at me. *Something good is going to happen,* I told myself, *I just know it.* And sure enough, the very next day, a most fortunate thing happened. Sister, Chi Haw, and their four little girls arrived in Shanghai. It was a happy reunion with Sister and Nieces.

That summer, counting the owners of the house, there were eleven of us living in those two rooms. Sister did the cooking, and I spent most of my days watching the little girls. When it got too noisy, I would take my nieces to the canal to sit on the bank. I told them stories about ghosts and brave little girls. Often Nephew would come along, and we all would play in the water and laugh. But never did Nephew and I laugh as hard as we had the day that I arrived in Shanghai.

Although the Communists had taken Chi Haw's land, Chi Haw had brought enough money to Shanghai to buy food, so we were never hungry. The little rooms at the top of the stairs got dreadfully hot that summer, but I didn't mind. I was glad to be with Sister and her little girls. At night, when we all lay down to sleep, we were like sardines in a very small tin.

That autumn we watched the leaves change from green to yellow to orange to red to brown. When every leaf had fallen from the trees, word came from Brother, news that would again change everything. One warm afternoon in late October, as I climbed the stairs with a jug of water, I heard cross words between the women. Once inside I saw Chi Haw's scarlet face. He scribbled on paper, pushed it in Sister's face, then pounded his fist on the table.

"Chi Fa," said Sister, pointing to her girls, "take your nieces for a walk."

Obediently, I helped the little girls down the stairs. As we went, I heard the women continue their angry exchange. "Having *him* along is too dangerous. He will get us all killed. Don't you see? A deaf man will bring attention to us," said Sister-in-Law.

"We must escape Communism, too," said Sister, "but I will not go without my husband."

"Don't you see, Chi Haw will cause us all to be arrested? Leave him. Come with us, and take your little girls to freedom."

By the time we reached the bottom of the steps, I could no longer make out their words. "Follow me," I told the little girls.

Flapping our arms wildly, like giant geese, we winged our way to the canal and landed on the bank.

Nieces liked to pretend. I leaned back and rested my head in the tall brown grass, and the little girls did the same. Practically as soon as the sun set, stars began to twinkle. I was puzzled by the angry words I'd heard. *Who is going, and who will be left behind? Where are they going? What will happen next?* I wondered.

When the little girls were tired of gazing skyward, we played tag. As I chased them in the moonlight, they raced about, falling and rolling in the grass in giggling fits. Hearing their happiness was my favorite sound—better than a cricket's chirp or even than the snoring song at Grandma's house. When it was time to rest, I said, "Before we go home, we have to spot a shooting star."

We all gazed skyward again, but I was the only one lucky enough to see a shooting star that night. After a few more silent moments beneath the milky sky, we lined up single file. Flapping our wings again, home we went.

Upstairs Chi Haw was standing in one corner with his back to everyone. Sister was reassuring him with a gentle touch. Her slightly raised hand told me not to ask questions. No one spoke. When it was time to go to sleep, I helped the little girls pull their blankets over them, and I lay down next to Sister. Later I whispered to her, "Are Sister-in-Law and Nephew leaving?"

"Yes. They are going to take a train to Canton and then go on to meet Brother," Sister whispered.

"And so are you, Chi Fa. Tomorrow at dawn you will leave."

"Tomorrow?" I asked. I couldn't believe it would happen so soon.

"Yes," said Sister, "in the morning."

I whispered, "I will miss you and Nieces."

"I know," Sister said comfortingly. "We will miss you, too. But I will see you again someday soon."

"I am afraid," I told Sister. "Should I be afraid?"

"It is okay to be afraid sometimes," said Sister. "Fear warns you when something is not good. But this is good, Chi Fa. This is the best thing for you. Remember, you are lucky. Good fortune will find you."

Then Sister rolled over and put one arm over Chi Haw. I fell asleep listening to the season's last cricket chirping a somber song.

PART III

CANTON

1951

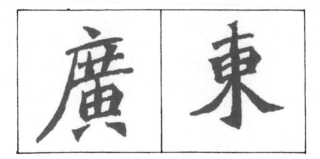

10
In the Attic
(Be Quiet)

Before morning's first light, I heard Sister-in-Law and Nephew stirring. I stood and rolled my thin blanket into a tight bundle. In the darkness, I stepped over the sleeping bodies of those we were leaving behind. I followed Sister-in-Law and Nephew down the stairs and into the street. I was sad to be leaving Sister, but there were no tears. She promised she would see me soon, and I had no reason to doubt her word. I could not have known, as we walked along in the hush of a rising sun, that it would be forty-five years before I would ever look upon Sister's face again. Instead of worry, wonder filled my head. *Will I ever have a home and roots and a place where I may stay forever and ever, safe and sound?*

It took the better part of the morning to walk to the Shanghai train station. Sister-in-Law set Nephew and me on a wooden bench and hurried off to buy tickets to Canton. We heard and felt it long before we saw it—a train! Its whistle split the silence of morning and warned all, *"Get out of the way!"* Then the ground rumbled and shook beneath us as it roared in like a giant iron tiger. With a weather-beaten face and squealing claws braking on the steel rails, the train rocked the earth and roared to a standstill. Resting in the station, the big rusty engine puffed great bellows of smoke. Nephew and I sat with our mouths agape, our hands covering our ears, and our eyes dancing.

We watched people getting on and off the train until finally the great doors clanked closed. The whistle blew again: *"Get out of the way!"* The train chugged down the track like a huge cat building speed, crashing metal, clanking rails, until it was only a dot on the horizon. Then it finally vanished. Nothing was left but the great puffs of steam that hung in the air thick like clouds over the tracks. My heart was racing in my chest. The train was the most powerful thing I had ever seen.

With three tickets in hand, Sister-in-Law returned. She sat on the bench between us, and in a low whisper she warned, "We're going to face a lot of uniformed men who are going to question us. No matter what you are asked, your only answer will be, 'I don't know.' Don't say anything. Don't give them any information. You don't know where you are going or from where you have come. Just nod and pretend you do not understand the words you hear."

I was nervous and anxious, but at last our train arrived. Sister-in-Law did not have to worry about me saying the wrong thing to the guards. I was so awed by the powerful locomotive that no words would come out of me. I boarded the train and sat in a seat by a window. I was so excited, I could hardly sit still.

For two days and nights, I stared out the window as bamboo trees and farm fields whizzed by. Only in my dreams had I ever imagined moving at such a great speed. As the train slowed before coming into each little station, I could see small huts and houses off in the distance. Once in a while I would see scattered cows or sheep grazing in a field.

At each stop, Communist guards came aboard the train and walked up and down the aisles, peering into the faces of the passengers. Sister-in-Law said they were trying to read fear in our eyes, so whenever a soldier looked at me, I lowered my eyes and thought about something else, like petting Spring Flower or playing tag with my nieces.

The clickity-clack, clickity-clack of the train on the tracks sounded good to me. It reminded me of the New Year's parade in Shanghai. There were no paper dragons or fireworks in the sky, but still the train ride was the most exciting thing I had ever experienced. Even a dragon dream could not compare to riding on a train!

Early on the third morning, we reached Canton. With my bundle in hand and a hope-filled heart, I stepped down to the platform. At first it was hard to get my legs to work. They felt weak, like half-cooked noodles. The ground seemed to pull down hard. After two whole days and nights of being hurled forward through space, it took some time to get used to standing still.

First thing, we walked to a special spot at the station where we were to meet a man that Sister-in-Law called a coyote. She said he was called a coyote because he helped people escape Communist China. Nephew and I weren't told any details of the escape plan. All I remember about the first day in Canton was standing and waiting. We didn't move from the spot where we were to make that connection. Trains came and went, people got on and off the trains, but still no one came to meet us. When the red sun slipped out of the blue sky and turned the world smoky gray, Sister-in-Law led us away from the train station. We walked to a little hotel, where she rented us a room.

The next afternoon, and the next and the next, Sister-in-Law went out searching for our connection. Every day she came back to the hotel with supper but no news of what we would do next. I wondered, *If she doesn't make the connection, does she have enough money to buy tickets back to Shanghai?* I had a nagging fear that if she needed money she might again sell me and take Nephew to safety. More than

once that week I had terrible nightmares about the
Communist parents.

Since I didn't completely trust Sister-in-Law, I
was very glad on the seventh day when she returned
with three train tickets and good news. She had
been approached by a man and his wife who
promised to help us escape to Hong Kong. We were
to take a late-night train to a nearby village. Twice I
counted the tickets in Sister-in-Law's hands to make
sure there was one for me. One. Two. Three.

As if in celebration of our good luck, the full
moon seemed to fill the whole sky. After a short late-
night train ride, we arrived in a tiny village. The man
Sister-in-Law called the coyote and his wife met us
at the station. Walking behind them, Nephew whispered, "Can we trust these strangers?"

"They are our only hope," she whispered back.

We followed the couple down a leaf-covered
path. I remember thinking how much they looked
like real coyotes. They were both tall and lean and
had short-cropped gray hair. They moved along the
path of brown leaves without making a single
crunching sound. I tried to walk without crushing
leaves beneath my feet, but I could not walk as
silently as they did.

Shortly, we reached a little two-story hotel with a
flat roof where the coyote had a deal with the hotel
owner. We went inside and waited on the first floor
until the coyote was sure no one was watching.
Then he took us past the reception desk, down a

hall with two tiny rooms on either side, and up a narrow wooden staircase. When we reached the small landing at the top of the stairs, we stopped and waited again. He listened. When he knew no one was watching, we went on. At the far end of the landing was a wooden ladder that went up to the roof. A door on each side of the landing opened into large storerooms. He opened the door to the store-room on the right, and we followed him inside. In the back of the storeroom was a door hidden behind some shelves. He opened the door that looked like shelves and behind we were very surprised to see a large attic where a group of people sat quietly, on blankets, on the floor.

The coyote said practically everyone in the vil-lage of two hundred knew each other. "Strangers are easily spotted on the streets," he warned. "You must stay hidden inside the attic and not go out on the streets or let the hotel guests on the first floor see or hear you." Then, without making a sound, he left us.

That night, and for the next two weeks, we lived and slept on the floor of the attic with thirteen strangers—all waiting to escape to Hong Kong. Nephew and I were the only children.

During the day we could move around quietly and speak in a whisper because the noise from the street below and the activity in the hotel kept the guests from hearing us. But as soon as it was bed-time, we had to sit or lie on the dusty floor of the large attic and not make a sound. We were warned

not to talk, sneeze, or even cough after dark. One
man snored every time he fell asleep, so his wife had
to sit up and shake him awake every time he began
his snoring. Because everyone in the attic was nervous that those below might hear us and turn us in
to the Communists, no one had patience with the
man who snored. I felt sorry for him and his wife,
who barely got any sleep.

In late afternoons, when I could sit still no
longer, I tiptoed down the hall and climbed the
wooden ladder that led to the roof. I crouched out of
sight and watched the people walking and bicycling
below. On one side of the hotel was a little theater,
and on the other side was an office building. Both
were one story high, so the people coming and going
could not see me on the roof. I liked to sit up there
and remember times when I could freely walk about
and come and go as I pleased. For a young boy, it
was hard to be quiet hour after hour. Often I thought
about the tag game I had played with my nieces that
last night in Shanghai. I missed Sister and her little
girls.

Each night at suppertime, the coyote's wife would
bring a large pot of rice to us. The woman shared the
rice as equally as she could, but always there were a
few who looked at the size of another's portion.

One night, after we had been there over a week,
the man, instead of the woman, brought up the pot
of rice. He explained that he needed to talk to
Nephew and me alone. Before we had even finished
our rice, he motioned with his arm for us to follow

him. We moved along the corridor to the end of the hallway, then climbed up the narrow stairway to the roof. We crawled through the small opening to the outside of the building. It was the middle of November and beginning to get cold. Night had fallen like a heavy curtain. "Follow me," he whispered.

We followed him to the far edge of the roof, at the back of the hotel. We crouched in a corner where no one looking up from the alley below could see us. He lit a cigarette. Blowing smoke through tight lips, he said, "Don't speak."

I found the brightest star and anchored my eyes. My heart was pounding. I knew the coyote had something important to tell us. When finally he finished his cigarette, he said, "I know you're young, but I am going to treat you like adults. During the escape, you can't make any noise. Even if you get hurt, don't make a sound." Then he put a hand over each of our mouths. "Just like this—not a sound," he said. I could smell tobacco on his fingers. As he removed his hands from our mouths, he said, "Everything will be okay as long as you don't make any noise. Understand?"

I felt certain the man was concealing something—something dangerous. By the look on his face, I knew his warnings were a matter of life and death. I was confident I could be still, but I wasn't sure about Nephew. For even now, Nephew looked as though he would break down and cry. I locked my gaze with the coyote's and nodded. Nephew nodded too.

"Escaping Communism is important to the grown-ups, but it's even more important for you two. You are still young and have your whole life ahead of you. You can stay and become a slave to Communism or escape and become your own man."

Nephew looked down at his feet, like he always did when he couldn't face something difficult. I wondered what Nephew was thinking. But more than that, I wondered what the coyote was remembering. This wasn't the first time he had helped people escape the Communists. I wanted to ask him to tell us what we could expect, but I knew he wouldn't tell us any more than we needed to know to survive.

Before we left the roof, he said, "If we are caught, under no circumstances are you to tell about the attic of this hotel. Do you understand?"

We nodded.

"Anything you say may result in the death of many people. You have to put away all childish things now and become men."

I squared my shoulders.

The next evening we had a break in the uneventful days. At twilight I was on the roof. A block away, I could see Communist guards in green uniforms hurrying along the street toward the hotel. The red stars on their caps flashed menacingly, and each guard carried a long gun. I climbed down the ladder as quickly as I could and warned everyone in the attic that the Communist guards were coming.

Sister-in-Law said, "Quick! Go back up on the roof. Take Nephew with you. Hurry! Go!" She pushed us out the door. The look on her face told me she was counting on me to keep Nephew safe.

We hurried along the corridor to the end of the hallway and then up the ladder. Without looking back, we crawled through the small opening to the outside of the building and onto the roof. We crouched in the corner at the front of the hotel, where we could peer over the edge and see the street below. We saw the uniformed guards pull about ten people from the hotel and tie their wrists together with rope.

When one man tried to speak, a guard hit him on the head with the end of his gun. The man fell to the ground, and the guard repeatedly kicked him. Wailing, a woman threw herself on the man's body. "Stand up and shut up!" yelled the guard who had done the beating. Grabbing the woman by her arm, he yanked her to her feet and shoved her back into the crowd. Then he kicked the man again.

The other guards laughed and talked. Some smoked cigarettes and flicked ashes onto the pavement. I tried to see if Sister-in-Law was in the line, but it was impossible to see the faces of those below. I listened as the guards asked a few of the prisoners questions. With each answer, the guards pushed and shoved the people.

After a while, several guards went back inside the hotel to search the rooms again. Suddenly there were loud bangs on the landing. The guards were in the storeroom. Had they found the secret door leading to the attic full of people? Would they climb the ladder to the roof and find Nephew and me crouching there? Would they drag us to the street and beat us too? My legs trembled with fear, and I sank to the floor of the roof, where I could no longer see the street, and waited. After many minutes, I heard the guards leaving the hotel. They lined up all the people, and at gunpoint they marched the prisoners down the street.

My knees were shaking so hard, I couldn't stand up. Crouched, I tried to draw the breath that was frozen in my chest. Nephew was crying quietly. I patted his head. We sat there for a while. Finally I stood and stretched out my hand to him. When he stood, he hugged me. In silence and nearly complete darkness, our friendship was sealed forever. Together we had survived. From that moment on, we were like brothers.

We felt our way back to the room where Sister-in-Law and the others were waiting. There wasn't a sound in the room. Everyone was in shock. For the rest of the evening, we were all a bundle of nerves. Later, in quiet whispers, we all said how thankful we were that we had not been caught.

After that night, we were all afraid we would be discovered and dragged into the street and arrested too. I longed for the time when we would make our escape. And soon my wish for action was fulfilled. Two nights later, the coyote brought news with our rice. "Tonight we leave. Here is the plan," he whispered. "Darkness is our friend. November's moon hardly glows. Now it is time to go."

A shiver ran down my spine.

D
O
U
B
L
E

L
U
C
K

He continued, "Tonight you are to go next door to the theater. Wear any extra clothes you have, but do not carry a bundle. Leave your blankets here in the attic. The movie begins at seven-thirty. After the movie ends, they will turn off all the lights in the theater. When you leave, use the theater's back exit, and meet me in the alley. By then the whole village will be dark." Then the coyote asked Nephew and me to repeat the instructions.

"When the movie is over, we are to leave by the rear exit and meet you in the alley," I said.

Nephew nodded. He looked as if he might cry.

"Do you remember what we talked about on the roof?" the coyote asked us.

We both nodded.

"I do not like taking chances. I should leave little boys out of this. If at any time you make noise or draw attention to us, you will be abandoned—left behind. Do you understand?" he asked.

We both nodded again.

After the coyote left, I thought about how unfortunate it was that I had to leave my blanket in the attic. It was tattered and worn, certainly not cozy and beautiful like Mama's quilt, but still, it had been my warmth for many nights. It had come the long journey with me from Shanghai—it made me feel safe. Carefully I folded the blanket and placed it on the floor. I thought, *I hope whoever finds this blanket will like it.*

Later that night, in small groups or pairs, all sixteen people left the attic and slipped next door to the theater. Sister-in-Law, Nephew, and I met a

Communist guard on our way to the theater. He
stopped us and asked Sister-in-Law, "Where are you
going?"

As if she didn't understand his words, she
squinted her face. There are many different dialects
in China, and each one is like a different language.
Sister-in-Law pretended she didn't understand the
question. If she had spoken, her northern accent
would have made the guard suspicious. She just
nodded and pushed us inside the theater. The soldier did not follow us inside.

We sat down in front, close to the screen, near
the back exit. I had never been to a movie before. I
wanted to enjoy the larger-than-life pictures and
sounds, but I couldn't concentrate. Nervous with
worry, I stared at the back exit and wondered what
was beyond that door. Would I be arrested and put
in prison for trying to escape Communist China?
Would I die at the hand of a Communist soldier? I
remembered the guards abusing the people on the
street in front of the hotel. I thought about how cruel
my Communist parents had been. How would the
Communist guards punish a small boy who was
caught trying to escape to Hong Kong?

After the movie, many left the theater. Those
from the hotel attic waited until the theater was
nearly empty, and then we left, a few at a time, by
the back exit. It was pitch dark in the alley. I could
barely see my hand in front of my face. We formed
a line and closely followed the coyote and his wife
to the edge of the village. There we took a narrow

dirt path lined with water chestnut and lotus fields. Carefully we walked along the mud-lined path for miles and miles.

After a few hours, the men felt sorry for Nephew and me, so they took turns giving us rides on their shoulders. We could not speak, but after the man who snored carried me for a while, I wanted to tell him, "When we are free, you will be able to snore as loudly as you want."

We walked half the night before we came to a river. It wasn't a wide river, maybe thirty or forty feet across, but it was very deep and icy cold. Most of us could not swim, so the coyote and his wife worked as human ferryboats and carried us on their backs, one at a time, across the river. The pace was frighteningly slow, but finally we were standing on the other side all together again. Wet and cold, we plodded forward in the safety of darkness.

After a few more hours, we reached an iron fence that was much too tall to climb over. It divided the Communist land from the English land. Standing on the Communist side, through twisted metal links, we could see freedom on the other side. Shivering from the cold, we all stood and waited as the coyote took out a pair of wire cutters and began cutting a hole big enough for a person to crawl through the fence. With each snip, the clippers made a loud snapping noise. To calm his nerves, the coyote took a break and lit a cigarette. What happened next was like a horrible nightmare.

The snap of the clippers, or perhaps the cigarette's red glow, alerted a pack of guard dogs. Their sudden, frenzied barking terrified our panicked group. Closer and closer the barking dogs came. Frozen in silence, staring into darkness, we waited for the hounds to pounce on us. Would they rip us apart or just hold us at bay until the guards could shoot us? I could hear men's voices from somewhere beyond. Within seconds, the night sky was ripped by the sound of machine gun bullets whizzing right over our heads. The guards had found us—we were going to die. My heart jumped into my throat. I crouched, my body shuddering from fear, and a sob leaped from my chest. I remembered the coyote's warning and put both my hands over my mouth. *Not a sound. No matter what happens, don't make a sound*, I told myself.

Knowing without a doubt that my last hour was at hand, I shut my eyes tight. Another sob leaped from my quaking heart, leaving a place for fear's long dagger. Terror stabbed at my chest—deeper and deeper until I could not draw a breath. For the first time in my life, it occurred to me that I might have to endure torturous pain before they would let me die. I imagined how it would feel to have a dog's jagged teeth rip open my belly or a bullet explode inside my head. I was a child! What did I care about being free? Why did I have to die like this, wet and cold, in the woods, in a battle that I did not start or even understand? My closed eyelids could not dam the salty tears that gushed down my face and stung my cheeks; I was too numb to wipe them away.

Pictures flashed inside my head—a whole life in a quick minute: Sister. Grandma and baby lamb. My friend sitting at his window. Butterflies and sweet peaches. A train roaring down a rusty track. Starry skies and full moons. Mama's quilt. I could see them all as clearly as the movie pictures in the theater.

No one in the group moved for what seemed like forever. It was a long time before I noticed that the machine gun fire sounded slightly higher overhead. Then as suddenly as they had begun their barking, the dogs stopped.

I opened my eyes. I could hear the men and dogs moving out into a clearing away from us. I was certain the sound of my pounding heart would bring them all back—the barking dogs, the guards and their guns. I listened. I waited. I listened and waited some more. And after what felt like an eternity, the men and the dogs disappeared. In the silence that followed, we all drew long, quiet, precious breaths of life.

The coyote was the first to move. When he thought it was safe, he finished cutting the hole in the iron fence and crawled through to the other side. Painstakingly he pulled us, one at a time, from the Communist side to the English side. It was nearly dawn by the time he pulled the last man through the hole.

When everyone was finally on freedom's side, the coyote smiled and motioned us with his hand to

follow him. And so we made our way up the slope
toward the skyline until we reached a road. It was
there that the coyote's sensitive ears caught the hum
of an approaching car. I didn't hear it. Wet, cold,
hungry, and scared, it was as though I were living in
a nightmare.

The coyote made a quick decision and divided
the sixteen people into two groups. I was with the
man's group, and the wife took a group that included
Sister-in-Law and Nephew. The two groups were led
off in opposite directions. Had I come all this way to
lose my family now? I stayed on the coyote's heels
and kept walking—one foot in front of the other.

Although it was daybreak, we were well hidden
in a heavy, dense cloud that touched the ground
like a thick mist. We walked until the sun, a ball of
fire, began to burn through the fog, and eventually
we reached a tiny bungalow. I followed the coyote
into a small room painted cloudy white. Exhausted,
I leaned heavily against the wall and slid to the
floor. I looked around at all the faces—faces as
white as the walls. We were all scared and too terrified to sleep. It was a long time before I stopped
shaking.

Quite a while later, Sister-in-Law and Nephew
arrived with the other group. I was so relieved that
we were all together again, I jumped to my feet and
ran to them. Warm tears of joy rolled down my face.
Relieved to be safe, we held each other for a long
time. Even though Sister-in-Law had sold me to the

Communist parents and Brother had beaten me, this was the only family I had now.

Still damp and cold, with only the relief I felt in my heart to keep me warm, I curled up in a little ball and tucked one arm under my head. I closed my eyes. I heard a man snoring loudly. Then I fell asleep.

PART IV

HONG KONG

1951–1952

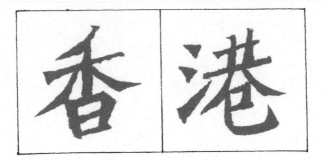

11
On the Island

(Be Unselfish)

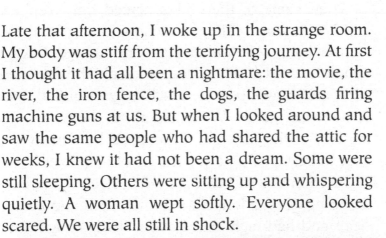

Late that afternoon, I woke up in the strange room. My body was stiff from the terrifying journey. At first I thought it had all been a nightmare: the movie, the river, the iron fence, the dogs, the guards firing machine guns at us. But when I looked around and saw the same people who had shared the attic for weeks, I knew it had not been a dream. Some were still sleeping. Others were sitting up and whispering quietly. A woman wept softly. Everyone looked scared. We were all still in shock.

The coyote's wife cooked rice porridge and boiled tea—hot, strong tea. "It will warm you," she said, passing out steaming cups of tea and bowls of porridge.

It tasted good, the porridge and the strong tea. I could have eaten a double portion if there had been enough. The aroma of food woke all those who were still sleeping, except Nephew.

For the first time, the coyote was friendly. I could tell he felt proud about getting us safely onto the English side. He said he had never come so close to being caught. "It was too dangerous," he said. Later he told us that he and his wife were going to stay on the English side and never take that chance again. To me, the coyote said, "You were courageous, Chi Fa. You kept up. You didn't make a sound."

I squared my shoulders. Nephew woke up just then and rubbed his eyes. He looked at the coyote and waited for his compliment. "You did well, too," the coyote told Nephew.

Then some of the others agreed that Nephew and I were brave. The man who snored patted me on the back. After that, everyone started talking about the dogs and how deep and cold the river had been and how close the machine gun bullets had come to our heads. We talked about the escape for the rest of the day. We all realized how lucky we were to be alive. We owed the coyote our lives.

As soon as it was dark, I tried to sleep again. Like dropping down a long dark tunnel, I fell into a fitful sleep and had nightmares about being caught and shot by the Communists.

The following day, in early afternoon, Brother showed up. Sister-in-Law and Nephew ran to him. I went to the coyotes and told them goodbye. With

money that my mother's youngest sister had sent
him, Brother paid the coyote for our freedom, and
we left.

From that point on, we were free. We walked a
short distance, then took a bus to the dock. When
we got off the bus, there it was—the East China Sea!
I was standing on the edge of the world. As far as I
looked, there was nothing but blue sky and ocean.

We took a ferry to a small, independent island—
part of Hong Kong that wasn't controlled by the
Communists. On the island, people were accepted
from all parts of China and placed in certain areas,
depending upon which province they were from.
Brother took us to Area Number Five. It was something like a military barracks. The houses were
made of heavy paper. People slept all together. Family members slept next to each other, but families
were mixed with many, many others. After showing
us where we would sleep, Brother guided us down
the hill to a church. "Every Saturday night I go to
church," said Brother.

That news surprised me because I didn't think
Brother was interested in church. Hungry and sleepy,
I tried to sit straight on the hard, wooden bench and
listen to a man talk about being thankful. I felt
thankful—very thankful that I was free and safe
from the Communists. Then everyone sang songs.
On our way out the door, the missionaries gave each
of us a big apple. Tromping back up the hill, crunching the sweet apple, I thought, *Now I know why
Brother goes to church every Saturday night.*

Back in Area Number Five, I spent my first night on the island with only a sheet to keep out the tropical winds that blew through the paper walls of the building. There was no privacy, but we were free. There was no food, but we had hope.

The next morning, Brother explained that the first people who had escaped to the island were given meal tickets by the government. Each family received a ticket according to the number of people in the family. Twice a day, people took their meal tickets to a nearby kitchen to get food. "Where's our ticket?" asked Sister-in-Law.

"There is more to this situation," said Brother. "Because so many people have come to the island, the government has stopped giving out meal tickets. They are not sympathetic to a man without a family, but perhaps with a wife and two little boys, my luck will change."

Picking up an empty five-pound milk can, Brother told us to follow him. As we walked, I paid close attention to the path we took so that I would be able to get back to the place where we slept.

The building where they gave away the food was a kitchen with a tiny pass-through window and one back door. We stood in a long line most of the morning. When finally we reached the window, Brother held up the can and began to tell our story.

"This is my family. They just arrived here last night after escaping from Shanghai. They have not eaten in three days," he lied.

"Where is your ticket?" asked the woman at the window.

"We do not have a ticket today," said Brother. "But tomorrow we will get one."

"So sorry, but I cannot give you rice without a ticket," said the woman working at the window. "Those are the rules."

But after being refused rice, Brother would not leave the window. He stubbornly stood there, giving one excuse after another. Soon the people in line behind us began pushing and shoving and calling Brother names. "I won't go until I have rice for my family!" shouted Brother.

With that, the women simply slammed the window shut in Brother's face. By then everyone in the line was irritated, and they yelled bad words and shook their fists at us. Many commanded Brother, "Get out of the line!"

But Brother wouldn't budge.

Shortly, the window flew open again. This time a different woman was there. She poked her finger out the window and wagged it in Brother's face. "We cannot give you rice without a ticket," said the woman. "Don't you understand Chinese? Go away!"

Still Brother stood firm. It was clear to everyone that he was not leaving the window without rice. Eventually those in line began shoving and pushing, and several of the bigger men used their hands to bulldoze the four of us out of the line. Brother knew he could not fight them all.

Red-faced with anger, Brother turned and walked away. Sister-in-Law and Nephew followed in his footsteps. I ran up to him and said, "Brother, give me the can. Let me stay and see if I can beg a bit of rice from each person in line."

Without a word, Brother handed me the can.

"Good luck," said Sister-in-Law.

With great hope, I went and stood close to the window. As each person got his portion of rice, I begged for a few grains. "Please, can you spare a bit of your rice?" The whole morning I stood begging, but not one person gave me a share of his meal. They were all hungry and wanted every grain of their rice.

When the sun was straight overhead, the window was slammed shut tight. Some in line did not get their rice that morning, but they did not go away. Instead, each sat down where he had stood and waited, where he would be one of the first in line when again the window was opened. I didn't know what to do, so I sat near the window and waited, too.

I searched the sky for dragon clouds, but every cloud I saw looked like a snake. In Chinese culture, snakes are not signs of good luck, like dragons, but are bad-luck signs. So when I saw a sky full of what looked like squirming snakes, I told myself, *Little dragons, lots of little dragons.*

Later, a big truck with armed guards came to the back door of the kitchen. Someone inside the kitchen unlocked the door, and the guards unloaded more food. Even before the truck had finished unloading

the supplies, the line began to grow long again. Hungry people waited by the hundreds.

After the back door was locked and the truck
drove off, the window opened once again. This time,
a big sweet potato was passed out with each portion
of rice. But after the sun had slipped halfway down
the sky, the window was slammed shut for the day,
and still my bucket was empty. I remembered the
pig's food that Aunt had fed me. Even that would
have tasted good then. I had hoped to please Brother
and surprise my family with their supper. Now I
could only go back empty-handed.

After the last person had gone, with my head
hung low, I turned to start back. It was then that I
heard a quiet voice say, "You, boy, come here."

A woman peeked out the window of the kitchen.
"Come around to the back door," she instructed.

When I went around to the back, she unlocked
the door and opened it wide. She asked, "Will you
help me?"

"Yes," I said.

"I cannot pay you," she said, handing me a great
straw broom.

She and two other women were wiping off the
long counter where they had measured the rice
before they cooked it. They pushed the rice that had
spilled from the measuring cups onto the floor.
Keeping my eyes on the big white grains that fell, I
swept the whole kitchen. And when I finished, there
was a big pile of dirt and sand—and mixed in the
dirt was rice.

"Clean it up," she said, smiling.

I bent down and, using my hands as a scoop, I picked up the pile and put it in my can. There was a nice pile of rice mixed in with the dirt—enough to feed four people. I wanted to hug the woman who had given me the job of sweeping. Instead, I rushed up to her and handed her back the broom. "Thank you very much," I told her.

With my great prize in hand, I hurried along to find my family. Halfway back, I remembered the beating Brother had given me in Shanghai for "dirty" rice. I didn't know what to do, so I sat down on a large, flat rock to think. In the end, I decided that Brother would not look past the dirt and see supper. So I poured out the contents of the can on the rock. Carefully I separated each grain from the dirt and polished it on my shirt. By the time the sun had completely disappeared for the day, I had a can half full of shiny, white rice. Feeling proud, I hurried back to Area Number Five.

If Brother was impressed with my ability to get rice, he did not show it. When I got back, he peered into the can and said, "It took you all day to get this little bit of rice?"

The next morning, when he sent me back to the kitchen to beg for food again, he said, "Try to get a little more today than you did yesterday. What you got yesterday was hardly enough."

The rest of the winter and most of 1952, the year of the dragon, I begged for rice at the window. The women in the kitchen liked me. I would put my little

can under the ledge where they passed out the
cooked rice. Purposely the women would make
messes on the ledge so that I could have the rice
that was spilled.

As I stood near the window collecting the spilled
rice and scooping it into my can, I talked to the
women. I told them the story about how I was given
the name Double Luck by the Communist parents. I
told them about Grandma and her lamb Spring
Flower, about my friend with the affliction, and how
I got to Shanghai.

"Oh, Chi Fa," they would say, "we are glad to
know a boy like you."

Soon I decided it would be easier to carry the
can back and forth to the kitchen if it had a handle. I
made a bucket from the five-pound dry-milk can by
poking two holes in the rim and knotting a piece of
wire through both holes. I also used the bucket to
get water for my family. Although we were on the
sea, we could get freshwater by digging a hole about
two feet deep in the sand and waiting until freshwater slowly seeped into it. Each morning, before I
went to beg for rice, I would dig a deep hole in the
sand and scoop up freshwater in my little bucket
and carry it to Brother.

On most days I could get my bucket three-quarters
full of rice—enough to feed four people. When I was
lucky enough to fill my bucket to the top, I sold the
extra rice for nickels. With the nickels I could buy
slices of roasted pork fat from a vendor. A thin slice
of the roasted fat was a nickel. A medium slice was

ten cents. And for three nickels, I could buy a big thick slice. This pork fat we used to flavor our rice—it was considered a big treat.

One night, after we had been on the island for a few weeks, I was curled up on the floor with the many strangers sleeping nearby. I heard a whispering voice say, "Chi Fa, you are very good at begging. You do it every day and feed your whole family."

"Thank you," I said in the darkness.

It is difficult to recognize a whispering voice, so I did not know who had spoken to me. I thought about the message all the next day. When I went to bed that night, I heard the whispering again. "Chi Fa, I see that sometimes you have more rice than your family needs. I was wondering if, on the days when you have extra rice, you would share it with me?"

"Who are you?" I asked. But the whispering voice said no more. As I lay awake wondering about the voice, I remembered what the very old man had told me: "In caring for others, I am serving heaven."

I wanted to help the person who needed rice, but I didn't know who he was. On the third night came more whispering. "I have two sons living in America. If you will share your rice with me, someday I will be able to repay you."

"No," I said in the darkness, "you do not have to promise me anything like that. From now on, I won't sell my extra rice. If I have extra rice, it will be yours. We are all hungry. We must help each other."

The next morning, the big smile on his face told

me who needed my rice. The voice turned out to be that of an old man who slept near me. From that day on, each day I gave the old man my extra rice. He was grateful for it. Over and over he said, "You are a good boy; you are like a son to me."

We quickly became close friends. He was old and gray, but he stood straight, not stooped like Grandma or the very old man who had given me the many cakes. We told each other stories at night. Often those who lay close to us would say, "Hush, we are trying to sleep."

So the old man and I would get up and go outside. We'd sit on a stoop and gaze up at the stars and moon. My friend knew many stars by name. With an outstretched arm he'd point to the Orphan Star and the Golden Star. He taught me how the moon rises nearly an hour later every night until finally the new moon comes up about the same time as the sun in the morning. He explained how the first quarter moons rise at noon and set at midnight and that the last quarter moons rise at midnight and set at noon—thus are visible during the day. He taught me about the seasons and how the planets revolve around the sun. He taught me many things about the sky.

The old man knew all about America, too. His sons wrote him letters. "America," he told me, "is a land of plenty. In America people eat three times a day. In America they are too full to swallow sorrow."

I could not even imagine such a thing—eating all I wanted. "Tell me more about America," I would beg.

"In America people live in houses with many rooms. Men drive their own cars, and little children own bicycles," he said.

One midsummer night the old man told me something I would never forget: "If a boy can catch the Orphan Star in the sky before any of the other stars begin to twinkle, and he makes a wish, that wish will come true."

After that, on the evenings when he caught the Orphan Star in the sky, the old man would whisper, "My sons are going to send for me soon. Maybe tomorrow."

Then one crisp autumn night, when the full moon looked like a silver apple hanging in the sky, the old man had news. "My wish has come true; my sons have sent for me; I am going to America," he said in one long breath.

He took out an envelope and showed me his airline ticket. Then, carefully putting the ticket back into the envelope, he thanked me for feeding him for so many months. "You saved me from starving," he told me as he pushed the ticket deep into his pocket. "I will never forget you."

As I sat on the stoop that cool autumn night, next to the old man, a warm feeling of hope began to swell inside me. I could have sat there, by his side, under the moon like that forever. It was peaceful. Finally, when he rose to go to bed, he whispered, "I promise you this: As sure as the planets have orbits, someday you also will see America."

The next afternoon, when I came back with my bucket full of rice, the old man was gone. Our friendship had been as sweet and cherished as the apples and oranges I received each Saturday night after church. Never before had I known someone else who liked to look at the sky the way I did. I was going to miss him, but I was glad the old man's wish had come true.

In midwinter, Brother decided we must leave the island. "There is no hope here," said Brother. "For over a year now, every day has been the same: eat and sleep, eat and sleep. We must go to a place where there is work." Then Brother told us his plan. "Each day we will sell any extra rice that Chi Fa gets. When we have enough money, we will take the Star Ferry to Kowloon."

Since I no longer gave the old man my extra rice, within a few weeks we had the coins we needed for the ferry tickets. I rose early the day we were to leave and went to the kitchen to say good-bye to the women.

"I will miss you, Chi Fa," said the woman who was in charge of the broom.

"I will miss you, too," I said. "You have been very kind to me. I will never forget you. I promise."

12
Beggar Boy

(Be Humble)

Hong Kong is a 400-square-mile colony, which was at that time owned by Great Britain. It is divided by the ocean. On one side is Victoria and on the other side is Kowloon. When the Communists took over China, the British government was required to hand over the Kowloon Peninsula to China. Only the Kowloon Walled City remained under British rule. That is where we were headed.

Our coins bought us seats on the lower deck of the Star Ferry. Filled with hope, I told myself, *I am riding a star to a brighter life.* I had no way of knowing then that the begging I had learned on the island would only prepare me for the years of panhandling that awaited me in Kowloon.

When we arrived, Brother soon discovered that there was no work of any kind available. Sister-in-Law couldn't speak the local dialect, so no one would hire her, either. The only way we could eat was for me to beg on the streets. At first I begged for rice, but I didn't often have good luck asking for food. Soon I switched and began begging for money.

In 1953, the year of the snake, I was twelve years old. Every morning, as soon as the sun was up, so was I. I went to the bus station where people stood waiting for buses. While they waited, I had an opportunity to tell them my story. I watched their faces as I began to speak. If there was no reaction, I knew they didn't understand the dialect I was using. Soon I learned to speak Cantonese, Mandarin, and Shanghainese; and of course I knew my hometown dialect. If a person did not understand what I was saying, I changed and spoke a different dialect.

"Double luck," I would say. "If you give this hungry boy a coin, it will be double luck. Lucky once because you will feed a starving child, and lucky twice because it will bring you good fortune. Heaven smiles on those who share with the poor. Please give me one penny—just one penny."

Often they would give me a coin, sometimes two. I kept the coins in my pocket, and before too long each day I would have collected enough coins to trade for three, or even five, Hong Kong dollars— about two or three quarters in American money. With this money, my family was able to rent a small wooden house that cost seven Hong Kong dollars a month. We had to cook outside. We had to bathe and go to the toilet somewhere else. But it was private, just the four of us—not hundreds, like it had been on the island.

By winter, I was skilled at begging, and Brother figured that we could double our income if Nephew would learn to beg, too. One day, when black clouds threatened rain, Brother said, "Take Nephew with you today. Teach him how to beg."

Obediently, I took Nephew to the bus station. I showed him the spot where I was luckiest at getting coins. "Take your hand and hold it like this," I said, showing him how to beg in a dignified manner. I told him what to say: "Feed a starving boy." Then I went around the corner and left him on his own.

When day ran into evening, the sky opened and poured down rain. I rushed back around the corner to see how Nephew had fared. Not only had the dark, dreary day disappeared, but so had Nephew and his empty pockets. After that disappointing day, he never again went to the streets with me to beg.

By springtime, I was getting enough money to feed the family and pay the rent, and some days there were even a few extra coins. Over several months, Sister-in-Law used the extra coins to buy enough rice to fill two big jars. The rice was our security—like having money in the bank. But no sooner had she filled the two jars than Brother began drinking rice wine and gambling more heavily. He liked to play mah-jongg, but he was not skilled at the game. By year's end, Brother had used all of our extra rice to pay off gambling debts. To keep my dying hopes flickering, each day I searched the skies for dragon clouds, and at night I watched the stars and moon. The sky gave me great comfort.

Once in a while I would gaze skyward and feel as happy as the sky was blue, and people can somehow sense when a boy is happy or sad. Beggars are not supposed to be happy. Beggars are supposed to be sad. One day when I was looking skyward and feeling a small measure of happiness, Brother came to me for gambling money. He asked, "How's your day turning out?"

"My day is good, Brother. How is yours?" I greeted him.

But he wasn't truly interested in my day. Brother only wanted the coins that I had collected. Sadly, I handed them over. When he discovered that I hadn't collected my usual quota for the day, he slapped me. Then he hit me with his fist, again and again. I crouched like a dog and put up my arms for protection. I screamed, "Please, someone help me!"

Fortunately, a man came to his window and yelled down to Brother, "What's going on? You shame yourself hitting a little boy. What reason could a man have for beating a child?"

"The boy is my brother. I will beat him if he needs it!" he shouted.

He struck me again and again. Soon some people

B
E
G
G
A
R

B
O
Y

gathered around to watch, and Brother was shamed away.

I was afraid to go home that night. Because I had caused him to lose face on the street, I knew that in the privacy of our house, Brother would get even. So I stayed on the street and begged some more. As it turned out, strangers are very generous to a boy with a bruised and bleeding face. I stayed until the moon disappeared behind black clouds and thunder rumbled in the distance. Then I cashed in all my coins for a five-dollar bill and hid the money deep in my pocket.

Afraid of the violent storm the sky promised, but even more afraid to go home, I made up my mind I would find somewhere else to sleep. At that time, there was a group of beggar boys who slept on the street every night, so I went where they slept, thinking I would be safe.

I curled up on the ground and fell asleep. That night, as the earth was softened by showers, I dreamed that it was raining coins from Heaven. In my dream I scrambled about, picking up coins as fast as I could. When my pockets were overflowing, I found a five-pound dry-milk can and filled it. Then I filled another milk can and another and another, until there were many cans filled with coins. At dawn, when I awoke, soaked to the bone, I wondered what such a dream could mean.

Discovering that my sudden riches had only been a dream wasn't my biggest disappointment that day. I reached into my pocket to get money to buy some breakfast porridge, only to discover that my five-dollar bill was gone. Someone had slipped it out of my pocket while I slept. So, without a bite to eat all day, I begged long into the night, until I had what I thought would be enough money that Brother would let me come home again.

PART V

TAIWAN

1954–1969

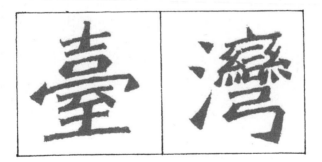

13
Auntie's House
(Be Hopeful)

期 盼

By the summer of 1954, the year of the horse, I was only thirteen, but I had been begging and supporting my family for nearly three years. With each long day of begging, hope's flicker grew dimmer. One day I looked at my tattered clothes and dirty, bare feet and realized that more than my clothes were ragged from begging. My spirit was worn, too. I longed for something more. Just then, an orange-and-blue butterfly landed in the palm of my hand. I watched it flex its wings open and closed before it flittered off. It was as though the bright butterfly had brought shiny new hope—I just knew that good fortune was on its way.

Within a week, the good news came. I learned from Brother that my mother's youngest sister had

arranged for us to enter Taiwan. Married to a representative of Jiangsu Province, Auntie was able to cut
through all of the red tape so that we could move to
the city where she lived. Auntie felt especially close
to Brother and me because she had taken our other
brother, Yeong Sheng, when he was born and had
raised him as her own son.

To get to Taiwan, we took an all-day ride on a big
boat called *Chung King*. Although my clothes were
ragged, I remember how proud I was to be wearing
boy's clothes and not the women's clothes and
bonded shoes that I had worn on the barge to
Shanghai. I remember something else very clearly,
too. There was a large mirror in the men's rest room.
The first time I saw myself in the mirror, I was very
surprised. *Who is that boy?* I wondered.

I hardly recognized myself. Gazing at my reflection, I squared my shoulders and stood tall. A good-
looking boy, not a beggar, stared back at me. For the
first time since I'd sat on the stoop, under the moon,
with the old man, hope glowed bright in my heart.
*Perhaps Taiwan will be a place where I may go to
school and be like the other boys—a place where I will
not have to hold out my beggar's hand and tell a sad
story*, I thought. I looked into the mirror and smiled
and saw a handsome Me smiling back.

In many ways, my hopes for Taiwan were fulfilled. It was a different world. Brother worked going
door to door selling cooked tenderloins from a basket. That meant I did not have to support the family
by begging. When school started, I was put in sec-

ond grade. Although I was small for my age, I was still much larger than the other children in my class. Many of my classmates laughed and poked fun at me, but I was determined to learn to read and write.

I was ashamed that I was uneducated, but I knew in my heart that reading was a skill I could master. Chinese symbols are not like words spelled with connected sounds. For each Chinese word, there is a different symbol. There were so many symbols to memorize, often I struggled. Sometimes Brother helped Nephew and me with our studies. When I could not read a word, Brother would hit me. "You are so stupid, Chi Fa. You are a big boy, and still you cannot do second-grade work."

Sometimes I felt like I could not go on another day, but I never disrespected Brother by speaking out. My thinking was this: *I was smart enough to beg for rice and money. I supported Brother and Sister-in Law and Nephew for many years. I could not read and write because I had always worked instead of going to school, but I could speak four dialects. Chi Fa was not stupid.*

If wanting something very badly could make it happen, I knew I could learn to read. *If only Favorite Uncle were here,* I often thought, *he would help me learn to read.*

At the end of the school year, there was a writing contest at school. Of the sixty-two students, three essays were chosen as the winners. When I went into the classroom and saw my paper posted as one of the three winners, it was a glorious moment. After six months of school, I successfully completed the work for second and third grades.

Early in June, 1955, the year of the sheep, Auntie sent for me. Brother Number Three, whom Auntie had raised as her own son, was grown and didn't live with her anymore. Auntie's husband, who worked for the government, traveled all over the world and was seldom home. So she was lonely and wanted the company of a boy. She longed to see her sister's little boy, Chi Fa. Brother didn't want to let me go because I did most of the work around the house— the cooking, cleaning, and laundry. But in the Chinese culture, the older a person is, the more power that person has. Auntie was older than Brother, so in the end, Brother had to let me go—but only for the summer.

Auntie's house was in a suburb of Taipei, a half-hour's bus ride from where we lived. The morning I left for Auntie's, I stood proudly at the bus station. I did not have to hold out a beggar's hand. I was going on a vacation.

When I got off the bus, Auntie was waiting for me. She knew me by my face. "Chi Fa, you look just like your brother, Yeong Sheng, when he was your age," she said with a little sob in her throat. I could tell by the look on her face that Auntie was happy to see me.

We talked as we walked to her house. Auntie lived in a big, fine house. As soon as we got there, Auntie told me I could have a bath. In her kitchen, behind the stove, was a big tub—big enough for a boy, or even a man, to sit in. She put on some large pots of water to boil. Then she had me draw water from her well. I carried in many buckets of water and poured them into the tub. Next she poured in the pots of boiling water. "Enjoy your bath," Auntie said, handing me a small cotton towel.

I had never had a bath in a big tub before. I was still staring at the tub when Auntie came back into the kitchen carrying a pile of clean clothes and a pair of shoes. "Here are some clothes that Yeong Sheng outgrew. I think they will fit you," she said, placing the stack on a small chair near the tub. Auntie left the kitchen again, this time closing the door behind her.

It was warm by the stove. I undressed and slipped into the tub of warm water. It felt too good to describe. In all my life, a bath has never felt better. As Grandma would say, "I washed away the cares of the day."

I stayed in the tub until the water was cold and my white fingers and toes were wrinkled like prunes. Then I got out and dried off and put on the nice clothes. No sooner had I finished dressing than Auntie knocked on the kitchen door. "Chi Fa, did you drown?" Auntie laughed.

"I am dressed," I told her.

When she entered the kitchen, she clapped her hands in glee. "Oh, Chi Fa, how handsome you are! Come outside on the porch and comb your hair."

I felt lucky that I got to go to Auntie's. It was a fine vacation. She didn't make me work hard, and she let me sleep until the sun's whole face looked over the hill. Each morning there was brown rice with toasted, salty peanuts waiting for me on the table in the kitchen. I had never had peanuts before. To make sure it was fair, Auntie counted the peanuts into our bowls. Every morning, we each got six.

After breakfast, we went outside to feed her many ducks. She'd count her ducks and call them all by name. If a duck did not lay its egg for the day, Auntie would scold it. "Bad duck. Lazy duck. Why didn't you lay your egg? Tomorrow I will cook you for supper if you don't lay an egg."

We would gather all the duck eggs, between twenty and thirty a day, and put them in a big basket. Auntie would count and recount them. Then she'd give me the basket to carry to Mr. Lo's Store. Auntie said, "Carrying eggs in a basket teaches a young man not to rush about."

Very slowly we'd make our way up the dusty dirt road. At Mr. Lo's Store, I'd set the basket, heavy with eggs, on the long counter. As Mr. Lo held up each egg to examine it in the light, checking to make sure there were no cracks, he'd grumble about the weather. "It's going to be another hot one," he'd promise. Or, "The wilted grass could use some rain," he'd complain.

Then Mr. Lo would weigh the eggs—he bought them by the pound. When there was one egg left in the basket, Auntie would say, "Not that one, Mr. Lo. That one's for Chi Fa's supper. He likes duck eggs."

After doing the figuring on paper, Mr. Lo would give Auntie a few coins for the eggs. Then we'd head straight to Auntie's house. With a nearly empty basket, the walk back seemed half as far as the walk to town.

Once back in her kitchen, she'd put the duck egg in a pot and cover it with water. She'd light a fire in the stove and put the egg on to cook. After the rice and vegetables were cooking too, she'd sit at the table and count the money she'd gotten for the day's duck eggs. Only after she was satisfied with the total would she put the coins in a blue jar that stood big and round in one corner of her kitchen. Removing the wooden lid, she'd say, "Come and see."

My heart would leap as I peered down into the big blue jar at the many coins. I thought, *Auntie is very rich*. Never in my life had I seen so much money in one place.

By then our supper would be cooked. She'd peel the egg and cut it in two, and we would eat the duck egg with our supper. Auntie always gave me the biggest portion of the egg. I quickly grew to love her. She reminded me of Grandma because she told me stories and listened to mine.

There were lots and lots of feathers in Auntie's yard. I showed her how to wash and dry them, then press them flat. I showed her how Grandma made little bouquets with feathers. We made all-white-feather bouquets, speckled-brown-feather bouquets, and colorful green-and-blue-feather bouquets. Soon

Auntie had duck-feather bouquets all over her house.

Every evening, as soon as it got dark, she'd say, "Chi Fa, let's go outside and count the stars."

We passed those precious summer nights on her porch, under the sky's splendor. Since Auntie's husband was a government representative, she knew all kinds of interesting stories about the world.

"Tell me about America," I would beg.

With a long sigh Auntie would begin, "In America, inside the houses, there is hot water that runs through pipes into big white porcelain tubs, and people take warm baths every day. In America, the children go to school and play instead of working all day."

Could such a place be real? I asked myself. Everything I had ever heard about America sounded almost too good to be true.

I told Auntie about the old man who had slept next to me on the island. I told her how he had told me stories about America and how finally he had gone there to be with his sons. I told her that he had taught me to name the stars.

"Knowing about the sky is a good thing," said Auntie.

"The old man believes that if a boy can catch the Orphan Star in the sky before any of the other stars begin to twinkle, and he makes a wish, that wish will come true," I told her.

Auntie gleefully clapped her hands. She leaned closer to me and whispered in my ear, "What is your wish, Chi Fa?"

"I have not yet wished upon the Orphan Star," I told her.

"Why not?" Auntie asked with a sigh.

"Because," I explained, "before I make a wish that might come true, I must be certain of what I want."

Gazing up at a single bright star shining through the darkness, again she asked, "What is your heart's desire, Chi Fa?"

I thought, but I did not speak or make a wish.

One night, as August's full moon rose big and bright, Auntie shared with me something special about Mama. "Your mother loved to read. She especially liked the writings of the ancient philosopher Confucius. She had a favorite passage," she said, standing and then disappearing inside.

When she returned she held a book. Placing it carefully, like a tiny baby, in her lap, she opened the book to a place that was marked with a ribbon. "Here," she said, tapping her long straight finger on the page. Then she handed me the book.

Very carefully I studied the beautifully written characters. Because I had gone to school, I could read each word. Proudly I recited:

> With coarse rice to eat,
> with water to drink,
> and my bended arm for a pillow—
> I have still joy in the midst of these things.

The next morning, before we collected the day's duck eggs, I copied Mama's favorite passage. I read it several times and then carefully folded the paper into a little packet and put it in my pocket. It would be safe there, and I could read it anytime I wanted to feel close to Mama.

I liked being at Auntie's house, but all too soon my time with Auntie was up. On the last night of my summer visit, I sat sadly on her porch. As if she knew my gloom, to cheer me, Auntie said, "Chi Fa, you are a good and handsome boy. I am proud of you. Your mother would be very proud of you, too."

"Thank you, Auntie," I whispered.

"Now," she said, pointing a straight finger at a lone star that twinkled in the sky, "there it is. Make your wish."

I gazed upward. Over the big moon, one star sparkled brightly. "I want to go to America," I whispered.

After that, neither of us spoke. We sat looking up at the white moon beaming down on us and listened to a choir of summer's crickets. *Oh, Auntie,* I thought, *I miss Mama and Sister and Grandma. Now I will miss you, too.*

The next morning, before I left to walk to the bus station, Auntie gave me a paper bag of salty peanuts to eat on the way home. With a bunch of her ducks waddling behind us, she walked me to the end of her road. Before she turned to go back, she squeezed my hand and said, "Chi Fa, when you look at the evening's first star and wonder if dreams come true, trust that they do." Then she hurried away, ducks quacking behind her.

14
Working for Mr. Yu

(Be Courageous)

勇 氣

When I got back to Brother's, my heart was full of hope, but as if to punish me for having a good vacation at Auntie's, Brother said, "Chi Fa, instead of going back to school, you must get a job."

His decision made me very sad, because I longed to learn how to read and write more words. For many days, I was miserable. Every day I took out the rice paper and read Mama's favorite passage. In the end I told myself, "I must accept things as they are rather than how I would wish them to be."

School resumed, but instead of going back to the classroom with Nephew, Brother took me to meet Mr. Yu, the manager of a construction company. Brother said that Mr. Yu needed to hire an office boy.

After we talked for a while, Mr. Yu said that he was impressed with my ability to speak many different Chinese dialects. "But most importantly," Mr. Yu said, "can you build a fire with charcoal?"

To me, that was not a problem at all. I had learned how to build fires with bamboo and straw when I lived with the Communist parents. I said, "Mr. Yu, I do not mean to boast, but building a fire is easy for me."

"Show me how you build a fire," he told me, pointing to the big iron stove in the middle of the office.

First I took some scrap paper from the trash can, wadded it up, and put it in the bottom of the stove. On top of the paper, I placed some wood chips that I found in a bucket by the stove. I lit them and carefully placed a few bigger pieces of wood on top of the flames. When I had a little fire going, I laid charcoal on top of it. After a short while, there was a nice warm fire with red-hot charcoal glowing white along the edges.

As luck would have it, Mr. Yu did not ask me if I had ever had a problem building a fire. I did not think it would be a good idea to tell him about burning down Grandma's hut.

"You're very good at building a fire, Chi Fa. It takes me many tries to do that." Mr. Yu hired me on the spot.

The construction company paid eighteen Taiwanese dollars a day plus overtime. That equaled about forty-five cents a day in American money. The construction workers earned the same amount as I, and their work was much harder than mine, so I felt very fortunate to have the office job.

After my first day on the job, Brother said he wanted to discuss business with me. "Chi Fa, it would be best if I kept your money and invested it for you," he said. "Someday, when you are a man, I will give it all back to you with interest. Then there will be enough for you to get a good start in life."

I wasn't even fifteen yet, so in my heart I knew I did not have a choice.

"Don't worry," Brother said. "I'm planning for your future."

From the very first day on the job, trusting that he would keep his word, I handed over all my pay to Brother.

My office job had many duties. I handled all kinds of business letters. Carrying them to the post office, buying stamps, and making sure they were mailed was my responsibility. It was also my job to buy small supplies and keep track of everything in the big supply room. Every man came to me to get his supplies. Men from all parts of China worked for the company, and since I had learned to speak Taiwanese as well as the other four dialects I already knew, I understood and got along well with everyone at work. Those were good days. I liked the work and was good at it.

Then one spring morning in 1956, the year of the monkey, when cloudy skies poured down rain, something terrible happened. Mr. Yu came in with a new broom for the supply room. I noticed that the receipt for the broom was for over six dollars. Without thinking, I blurted out, "Oh, Mr. Yu, you paid too much for this broom. I buy brooms at the store on the corner, and they cost only two dollars—under two dollars. You paid way too much."

Mr. Yu showed me a face that I had never seen him wear before. It was like a wild animal cornered by a hunter, waiting for the bullet. "How much I pay or how little I pay for supplies is none of your business," he snarled.

That night, curled up on my sleeping mat, as rain poured on our roof, I figured out that Mr. Yu hadn't paid six dollars for the broom. He had probably spent less than two dollars. Thinking back on other supply transactions, I realized that Mr. Yu and the accountant had probably made a deal. I figured they were splitting the difference between the true price of the supplies and the amount shown on the receipts. I did not know what to think or do about Mr. Yu and the accountant stealing from the construction company. Worry kept me awake the whole night.

Morning was gloomy, and so was I. As soon as I got to work, Mr. Yu called me into his office. Wearing a mean look, he told me that I was fired. At the word *fired*, my world collapsed from under me. I did not want to leave my job, but I was only fifteen years old. Mr. Yu and the accountant were grownups. Mr. Yu knew the power he had over me and knew that his word would be honored above mine. Humiliated and sad, I went home to face Brother.

However, as misfortune often does, it left another door wide open. With the help of a man named Koa, whom I had met in Mr. Yu's office, I found another job within a week. An American officer's club hired me as a busboy.

The club, in a suburb of Taipei, had a huge dining hall with a center stage. Most nights, Filipino musicians performed. On Wednesday nights, there was Bingo at the club. Each month I was paid six hundred Taiwanese dollars—about fifteen dollars in American money. It was a one-hour walk from Brother's to the club. Each day I left the house in the gray light of dawn and didn't return home until long after dark. My new job left no time for making friends, but working in an American club, I soon learned to understand the English language. Serving American officers each day intensified my desire to go to America. I thought of the officers as father figures. They looked proud and important in their uniforms, and I hoped one day to be respected like they were.

On American holidays, the club served big dinners, and the Chinese workers were fed, too. I quickly grew to like American foods. At first it was difficult to use American eating utensils: spoons, forks, and knives. I was used to eating with chopsticks, but with practice, I learned.

The American officers had trouble remembering all the Chinese workers' names, so one day at the club they placed a basket of name tags on the stage. Each tag had a different American name: David, John,

Richard, Robert—popular American men's names. We were all told to take a name tag and to wear it. I was the last in line, and by the time it was my turn to take a name tag, there was only one tag left in the basket. I picked it up and read, "Gordon." That's how I got my third name—my American name. And to this day, my American friends call me Gordon.

Many nights, after working all day, I would be tired and could hardly drag my aching body home. I could have ridden a bus for a nickel, but because I was saving for my future, I always walked home, unless it was raining. With only the silent moon to light my way, I would tell myself, *The pain of the body is nothing.* Putting aside all wishful thinking, I gave every cent I earned to Brother.

November 27, 1958, the year of the dog, was like no other day in my life. It was a day with a wrinkle in time—moments that stood still—and after that day, nothing was ever the same again. It was the American holiday called Thanksgiving. The club served a feast of American foods: baked turkey, mashed potatoes with gravy, cranberry sauce, and pumpkin pie. In all my life I had never seen that much food or so many dishes. When finally the last plate was put away and the floors were swept and scrubbed, I wearily walked out of the club into the night and headed home. Nothing but the scuff of my shoes on the ground broke the silence. The moon hung huge and lazy on the horizon, unconcerned by its upcoming journey across the sky.

It occurred to me as I walked along, alone and dog tired, *If I had a bicycle, I could ride back and forth to work. Yes, why not?* A bicycle was just what I needed. When I trudged into the house, Brother was still up and sitting at the table. Nephew and Sister-in-Law had already gone to sleep. I don't know what made me do it, but I asked Brother about my money. I said, "I need my money. I want to buy a bicycle."

"It isn't that simple," Brother said. "You cannot just have your money any time you want it."

I don't know where I got the nerve to ask for my money. I had never had the courage to ask Brother for anything before. Exhausted, I just knew that a bicycle was a good idea. I had worked hard and deserved to spend some of my money. "Every pay period for over three years you took my money," I heard myself scolding. "Tell me where it is being kept."

Calmly, Brother described a private savings system where he said he had invested my money. "Everyone involved contributes money, and once a month, there is a lottery to see which contributor will receive all the money. The lucky person who draws the highest number gets the full amount, and he only has to pay it back a little at a time. It's an opportunity to borrow money without paying interest. It is like a private bank without contracts—better than a bank because it works on trust," said Brother.

I thought, *This is my own brother. If I cannot trust my own brother, who can I trust?*

"How do you know that you can trust strangers?" I asked him.

"Everyone trusts everyone else in the group. Believe me, I know what I am doing. You have to trust me, Chi Fa," he concluded.

"You know, I had hoped that you were someone I could trust. You are my eldest brother, and I had convinced myself that you would protect my money. But now all you give me are excuses. I want my money tonight," I told him. "Tomorrow I want to buy a bicycle. I need a bicycle to get back and forth to work. Where is my money?" I asked again.

"You cannot get the money until you draw the highest number in the lottery," Brother said. He went on to give me one excuse after another. For quite some time I listened, but the excuses didn't match. I lost my patience. "I need my money now," I demanded.

"You don't have enough for a bicycle," he stated flatly.

I knew that was not true, and I lost my temper. "I don't believe you. I have been giving you more than six hundred dollars a month for three years. That is a big chunk of money. I want it, and I want it now!" I shouted angrily.

Raising one hand, he interrupted me. "Don't worry. You will get your money. I did all this for you, Chi Fa. You just have to wait until you are a man."

Always I had been afraid of Brother because he beat me when I was little. But suddenly I felt courage that I didn't know I had. "I am not afraid of you," I told him. My voice was shaking, but I went on. "I have scars all over my body from the sharp bamboo with which you beat me, but I am no longer afraid of you. I demand that you give me what is mine."

Brother didn't know what to say. He raised one arm as if to strike me, but he didn't stand or move from the table. I was now bigger than he was, and Brother knew it. "You will get your money back someday. Don't ask again. Be good and go to bed," he snapped.

I shrieked, "When I was a little boy begging on the streets and I brought home money, you were satisfied, but when I couldn't get enough money, you beat me. I have worked like a mule supporting this whole family for seven years and have handed over every penny to you."

"I have provided you a home and food to eat," he countered.

"No!" I shouted. "I paid the rent. I bought the food. I am the one who has provided for you. Your son, who is only one year younger than I, has never had to lift a finger to help the family. He is precious to you. I am your brother, but I am not respected. You make me your slave. Think about how you have treated me!"

With obvious effort to regain control, he recited, "I am thinking of you. I have been saving your money for you. Someday your money will all be there. You will thank me then. Trust me."

"I don't trust you!" I yelled. "You bled our father when he was alive. You dishonored our ancestors by gambling away the store that our grandfathers worked hard to build. Generation after generation of effort—you threw it all away on gambling debts. Now you are robbing me!"

He glared at me, hate blazing in his eyes. I was relentless. I could not stop myself from saying all the things that I had held in for so many years. Like hot, molten lava my outrage spewed. Brother clenched his fists. He was so angry he could not even speak. I continued, "I have tried all my life to please you. I had hoped to earn your gratitude, but there is no appreciation for me in this house." Red-hot anger rushed from my chest to my lips, and I shouted, "You are a liar and a thief!"

Instantly I regretted saying those words. My mind flashed back to Communist Mother's twisted mouth shouting, "Liar!" "Thief!" A sick feeling washed over me. It was true, Brother did not always tell the truth, and he wouldn't give me my money; but he was still my elder. I should not have disrespected him by calling him names. Brother's face sagged as though a dagger had stabbed him in the heart. His head collapsed in his hands.

I was old enough to know that when one is not the captain of his own words, he must go where his out-of-control ship takes him. I had launched myself on a new sea—this could no longer be my home.

"In the morning I will move out," I promised Brother. Leaving him with his head still in his hands, I silently slipped from the room and went to my sleeping mat. That night, noisy thoughts kept me from sleeping a wink.

15
My Own
Place
(Be Independent)

自 立

The next morning, before either the sun or Brother
was up, I packed all my belongings in an old wooden
box. To secure the box's lid, I tied straw twine
around it. I carried the box to work with me and set
it in one corner. That whole day, the box stared back
at me. What was I going to do? Where would I go? I
couldn't ever go back to Brother's.

In the late afternoon, I told my supervisor about
the fight that I had had with my brother. When I finished my story, he said he would advance me a few
dollars. He knew of a room for rent, and, with his
directions, I went there after work. The place was
just a few blocks from the club, one room with a
door facing an alleyway. Although I would have to

share a bathroom and shower, at the end of the alley was a clean courtyard with a faucet, where I could get good drinking water.

Those first days, I was too sick at heart to enjoy my new independence. I didn't want to live under Brother's roof, but I wished that our parting had been less painful. That first week, I spent my nights lying on my bed, staring at the ceiling, hardly sleeping. In the end, I decided that although the fight with Brother had been a dreadful ordeal, I might not have ever had the courage to leave if it hadn't happened.

On payday, with my money in hand, I went shopping. I bought a shiny new bicycle. It was beautiful. With great pride, every day I rode my bike back and forth to work, and at night I parked it inside my room right next to my bed.

After two more weeks, I received another check. This time, I bought a radio with big speakers. I can still remember how it soothed me to lie on my bed in the dark and listen to the music. Sometimes in the evening, when the girls were in the courtyard doing laundry, they would ask me to open my door and turn up my radio so that they could listen to my music too.

It was difficult to forget about that terrible night at Brother's, but I slowly began to feel better and to enjoy my independence. Playing my own music was part of my newfound freedom. I had a bicycle and could go places. I had plenty to eat at the club where I worked, and I had my own comfortable bed. I was free. After buying the bike and radio, I saved every penny in hopes of someday going to America.

About two months after I left Brother's house, Nephew knocked at my door. I was happy to see him and proud to show him my place. Nephew was impressed with my radio, but he liked my bicycle best. He didn't know how to ride a bicycle yet, so in the courtyard, with a handful of giggling girls watching, I held up the back of the wobbly bike and ran around behind him. Every time he lost his balance and nearly fell, we laughed.

The girls laughed too. I told them that my nephew was like a brother to me. "See him go!" I exclaimed.

Soon Nephew could balance and ride without my hand to steady him. I was proud of Nephew, but I also felt sorry for him because he had to live with Brother.

As Nephew was getting ready to leave, his glad face faded. He told me that Sister-in-Law was sick. He said that Brother had sent him to get money from me to pay for the doctor. I had no doubt that the story was true, so I gave Nephew all that I had saved.

On Chinese New Year's 1959, the year of the pig, Nephew came for another visit. As the sun turned the sky shades of orange and pink, we walked to the marketplace, where I bought us rice balls with black sesame seeds inside.

"Good fortune has found you, Chi Fa," Nephew said between savory bites of sweet rice. "You have your own place and a good life; I can tell."

"Someday you will have your own place, too," I said encouragingly. I wanted to tell Nephew that he was old enough to leave Brother's house now, but I did not think it was wise to advise him. Becoming independent is a decision a boy must make on his own. Only then can he become a man.

Watching the New Year's long parade of paper dragons weaving through the street, we recalled the New Year's parade we'd watched when we were little boys in Shanghai. The only difference was that no Communist soldiers carried Chinese Communist flags and posters of Chairman Mao. We agreed that we were fortunate to be living in Taiwan, the Free Republic of China, and no longer citizens of Communist mainland China. Under the night sky lit with fireworks' sparkling colors, Nephew and I celebrated my new independence.

Before he left, Nephew asked me for money again. And, of course, I gave it to him.

Over the next three years, Nephew repeatedly came to me, always telling me sad stories and leaving with whatever money I had carefully saved. Brother never bothered to come to see me. He never came to ask, "How is the food? Are you warm enough? Is there anything you need?" No, Brother only sent Nephew to me when they needed my money. Even though I was free from living in Brother's home, he still had a hold on my earnings, because I felt an obligation to my family.

The charity to Brother didn't end until December of 1961, the year of the ox. In Taiwan, all boys have to go into the military—it is not a choice. After one is drafted in Taiwan, honest answers to the government and a clear family background are more important than even one's education and skills. My family history was clean, and I tried hard, so I did well in the military.

After induction into the military, I lived on the base and was paid $1.75 per month. Not $1.75 per hour, per day, or even per week—$1.75 per month! I didn't have even a penny to spare. One good thing about being in the military was that I didn't have to give Brother money.

A very exciting part about being in the military was that I was sent to school to be part of the military police. Also, I had my first girlfriend while I was in the military. Her name was Golden Sun, but I called her by her nickname, Grapefruit. It seemed that every time I had a rough day in the exercise room or got into trouble because I could not do something, Grapefruit would show up with a picnic. We would get away where we could be alone, sit, and talk. She liked my stories and would listen with a smile. She made me feel good about myself in the same way that Grandma and Auntie had.

I was an MP until I was discharged from the military the first week of December 1963, the year of the rabbit.

16
Working for Mr. Ching
(Be Prosperous)

成 功

I didn't hear a word from Brother during the two years I was in the military—not even to ask for money. When I got out of the service, I lived in Taichung and wasn't eager to make the two-hour-long train trip to see him in Taipei. Shortly after I was discharged from the military, I received a disturbing letter from Auntie.

> *My Dear Chi Fa,*
>
> *You may receive the news that I am about to impart with mixed emotions. I have had news from your brother's family and have learned that your nephew is now married. They live in their own house, a house bought by your brother with your money.*

Although you can never reclaim what is rightfully
yours, be consoled by the fact that the money was
not squandered on frivolous pursuits.
      I hope you will come to visit me soon. I miss you.

                                    Fondly, Auntie

Auntie's letter opened an old wound. When I had left Brother's house, I felt certain that I would never get my money back. Still, it hurt to know that it was all together somewhere and I could not touch it. After a few days of reflection, I wrote to Auntie thanking her for the news. It gave me some satisfaction to know that Brother had not gambled away my hard-earned money. I liked my nephew, and I wanted him to be happy. Now, at least, I knew Nephew, his wife, and someday their children could live away from Brother.

My first civilian job after the military was as a waiter at Club 63, an American noncommissioned officer's club in T'ai-chung. I started working there just after the death of the American president, John F. Kennedy. I remember on my first day on the job, everyone in the club was talking about the assassination. Like the young American GIs, I was saddened by the tragic loss of President Kennedy.

As for my dream to go to America, I soon learned the truth. I could wish endlessly, but even if I could save enough money, it was nearly impossible for a young Chinese man to get the papers needed to go. One of the biggest obstacles was that the Taiwanese government would not allow men under the age of forty-five to leave the country. Would I have to wait more than twenty years to make my dream come true?

For the next six years, I worked as a waiter, maître d', chauffeur, and delivery man and took every odd job I could find. No job was too hard for me; usually I worked two jobs a day. Working with American GIs, I often heard stories about America, and although the dream seemed to get further and further away, with each passing day I longed more and more to go. I told everyone who would listen about my desire to go to America.

Luck seemed to be the prize for my patience. One day in the late summer of 1969, good fortune found me. A young Chinese man wearing a sad face came into the club while I was working and ordered coffee. "Why the long face?" I asked, setting his cup of coffee on the table.

"Just now," he told me, "I have come from Taipei. Yesterday I had to say good-bye to my best friend. He flew to America, and I will never see him again."

"I am sorry for you, but glad for your friend," I told the man. "Maybe you can go to America to see him," I suggested.

"Oh, no," he said, waving his hand, "I have no interest in going to America."

"Is your friend Chinese?" I asked.

"Yes," said the man, sipping his coffee.

"Is he a young man like you?" I asked, trying to hide my excitement.

"Yes. He is in his early twenties like us. Why all

these questions about my friend?" he asked, frowning over the rim of his cup.

"It has always been my wish to go to America," I told him. "My good fortune awaits me there." I knew he didn't want to hear about my dreams, so I tried to soothe him with kind words. "You can write your friend letters, and maybe he will come back to visit you someday."

I could tell he didn't want to talk about the details of his friend's departure, but I just had to find out more about how a young Chinese man had obtained the papers needed to go to America. "How did your friend get a visa and passport?" I asked.

"Well," he said with a long, sad sigh, "a man named Mr. Ching helped him."

I could hardly believe my ears. With a shaking hand, I grabbed his empty cup and went to refill it. When I got back to the table, summoning all my courage, I asked another question. "Exactly how did this Mr. Ching help him?"

"Go see Ching for yourself," he suggested. "He will tell you the details."

"Will you arrange our meeting?" I begged.

"I will try," he promised.

Then we talked about the weather.

Within the week, the man was back, this time wearing a smile. "I have arranged a meeting with Mr. Ching for you," he told me. "He lives in Taipei. He will see you early next Monday morning."

On Sunday afternoon, I took the train to Taipei.

The clickity-clack, clickity-clack of the train on the tracks took me back to my first trip on a train. I had been a boy then, a boy who did not know the dangers and hard path ahead of him. I was glad on that second trip to be a man—a man following his dream, and not a little boy running from the Communists.

I was nervous about being late for the interview the next morning, so to make sure that I would be able to find Ching's office without getting delayed or lost, I walked from the train station directly to the dock and located Mr. Ching's place of business. Only when I was sure of the way to get to the warehouse did I walk to Auntie's to surprise her with a visit.

Auntie was delighted to see me. It had been years since we had said our good-byes at her gate, but she had faithfully written to me while I was in the military. When she opened her door and saw me standing there, she clapped her hands with glee, "Oh, Chi Fa, come in. Come in!"

Hurrying around her dimly lit kitchen, she boiled a duck egg and chopped fresh garlic. She seasoned the crushed garlic with soy sauce and sesame oil and piled it high on top of tofu. She peeled the duck's egg and sliced me a big piece of tofu. As I ate her delicious meal, she shared news of my family. Sipping tea and smiling she remarked, "Chi Fa still has a big appetite." She clapped her hands again with glee, "Very good."

Later, when we were perched on the porch side by side, she told me how handsome I had grown and how proud she was of me. As a sliver of moon tried to break through a heavy cloud cover, we discussed the possibilities that awaited me at Mr. Ching's. "Mr. Ching is a link in a chain of events that will change your life forever," Auntie predicted.

The next morning, I rose way before dawn. Auntie wasn't up. Even her ducks were still sleeping. On my way through the kitchen, I found a small bag of peanuts on the table with a note: "My Dear Chi Fa, Good luck with Mr. Ching." I stuffed the note and peanuts into my pocket, and, careful to go quietly, I left the house and headed for the docks.

I was to meet Mr. Ching before the other employees came to work. Enjoying the salty peanuts, I hurried along the fog-covered dock to the big warehouse. I had no trouble finding Mr. Ching. The lights in his office glowed through the thick early-morning fog that had seeped into the warehouse from the outside.

I knocked softly on his open door and peered inside. Mr. Ching was at his desk. He looked up and smiled. A man in his late forties, Mr. Ching was soft-spoken. Sensing my nervousness, he invited me in, asked me to sit, and poured us cups of steaming tea from a pot on the big stove in one corner of his office. Nervously, I gulped my tea and looked around at the most elegant office I had ever seen.

Mr. Ching didn't waste any time. His first question was direct. "Why did you come to me?"

He sat back in his big chair and waited for my answer. Something about his soft voice and the way he intently studied my face made me feel comfortable. With growing confidence, I poured out my heart to this stranger. I told him that since I was a little boy, it had been my dream to go to America. I told him how I had tried to save, but how Brother had kept my money and then used it to buy Nephew a house.

Ching's face told me that he was listening with his heart. I told him about being in the military and earning only $1.75 per month. I even told him about being sold to the Communist parents for five hundred pounds of rice. When I had finished my stories, I was calm, and my second cup of tea went down more smoothly.

By the time the workers arrived and began filling the warehouse with noisy conversations, the sun was up and the fog was gone. Ching rose slowly, then walked around his office, turning off most of the lights. When he was finished, he came to me and shook my hand. With the warmth of his firm grip still radiating in the palm of my hand, Ching smiled and said something that made me very happy: "Okay, I think I can help you."

"What should I do?" I asked him.

"Well," he said, "about the only young Chinese men who are allowed a visa to go to America are those who work in the import and export business." Then he asked, "Will you come to work for me as a delivery man?"

"Yes, I will!" I assured him.

As we made our way through the warehouse, he proudly pointed out a few things. Standing in the open door of the warehouse, he said, "You must move from T'ai-chung to Taipei so that you will officially reside in the city where my firm operates."

With quick nods, I assured him that I would do that.

Back in Auntie's kitchen, over sticky rice and fried shrimp, I told her the details of my interview with Mr. Ching. When I had finished, she smiled. "Oh, Chi Fa, as sure as the sky is blue, your wish is going to come true."

That August night, as we sat on the porch listening to night sounds, we were surprised with a meteor shower. It was as though the sky were celebrating my good fortune. I told Auntie, "When I was a little boy and wished upon the Orphan Star, my fate appeared as fixed as that lone light hanging on the horizon. But tonight, my fortune is improving as rapidly as the shooting stars are streaking across the sky."

Before we went to bed, Auntie suggested that I come and live with her while I was working for Mr. Ching. The next day, I took the train home and went straight to work packing my belongings. I quit my jobs in T'ai-chung, and by the end of the week I was living with Auntie. Early the next Monday morning, I was on the job at Mr. Ching's.

Just a few weeks later, things began happening for me. After I gave Mr. Ching the necessary information, he helped me apply for a passport. I also needed a visa, and Mr. Ching made an appointment for me to visit the consulate. He took great care to tell me how I was to dress for the interview, and I had two blue suits made. He rehearsed with me what I was to say and instructed me to apply for a visa as a businessman.

The day of my interview, I put on a blue suit, white shirt, and blue tie. When I got there, although many others were being rejected, I remembered Mr. Ching's advice and stayed calm. The interviewer was a nice lady. Fortunately, my interview was successful and resulted in a visa.

Just a few short months after meeting Mr. Ching, I had both a passport and a visa. At last, I could make my plans to go to America.

In those days, a one-way airline ticket to America cost almost $350 American. Each Chinese person leaving the country was allowed to take at most $350. As soon as I had saved $700, I bought my airline ticket. I was nervous for days before I had to leave. I knew that I would be flying to another country and a new life, and that I would never be coming back. The week before I was to go, I spent every night stargazing on the porch with Auntie.

On October 29, 1969, the year of the rooster, I rose before dawn. As I prepared to leave Taiwan, like reviewing a scrapbook, I turned the pages of many departure days. Carefully arranging my few belongings in a suitcase with one of my two blue suits, I remembered how small and helpless I'd felt the gray day that Sister had left me standing alone at the door of Favorite Uncle's house. A cricket in a cage was all I had taken with me that day. In the years that followed, other family members had abandoned me, too.

Cold terror gripped me as I recalled being sold to the ironhanded Communist parents. Closing my suitcase and snapping the locks shut, I squared my shoulders and tried to shake away the feeling of defenselessness that had controlled my early childhood days.

Putting on a big smile for Auntie, I went into the kitchen for breakfast. Slowly chewing my rice porridge and peanuts, I studied Auntie's sweet face in the morning light. I knew it was going to be difficult to say good-bye.

While we sipped our last tea together, remembering a happy time, I told Auntie all about the day that Sister had come to the canal and saved me from the Communist parents. Then, without mentioning it to Auntie, I remembered the evening I left Favorite Uncle's and the dreadful night I had run from Grandma's burning hut.

After I finished my tea, I went to the bedroom to dress. Putting on my new blue suit, I was reminded of the morning I had dressed in women's clothes and bonded shoes to go to Shanghai. Remembering my epileptic friend, a tear leaked from my eye. As I left the room, I recalled stepping over Sister and Nieces, who lay sleeping on the floor in Shanghai. That had been over eighteen years before. Sister and her family never had come to Hong Kong, as she had hoped they would. Escaping to freedom was not to be for Sister, Chi Haw, and their four little girls.

My heart raced remembering my middle-of-the-night flight to freedom with the coyotes and those who shared the attic. It had been Auntie's money that had paid the coyotes for our freedom. I had so much for which to thank Auntie. With suitcase in hand, I went to find her.

She was sitting on the porch. I sank down next to her. Studying my sad face, Auntie said, "Chi Fa, it is better by far to forget and be happy than to remember and be sad."

Neither of us spoke for what seemed like a long time. The silence peacefully transported me to the stoop under the moon and the promise of the old man on the island: "As sure as the planets have orbits, someday you also will see America."

"Some of my memories are happy ones," I assured Auntie. "Many of my fondest childhood memories are of the days that I spent with you."

Too soon it was time to leave. Auntie walked me to the end of her road. She hugged me hard and said, "Chi Fa, when you see the evening's first star and wonder if I am thinking of you, trust that I am." Then she turned and hurried away.

I watched until she disappeared around the bend in her road, then I headed for town. The warm sun on my back, like a reassuring hand, pushed me along. Eyes skyward, I watched white puffy clouds gather around the sun.

When I got to town, I hailed a taxi to take me to the airport. The noisy, bumpy ride seemed to shake loose the unpleasant memories of the morning that Mr. Yu had fired me. Soon the feeling of humiliation was replaced with heartache as I recalled the terrible night that I fought with Brother. I trembled just thinking about it. *Auntie is right*, I told myself. *Some things are best forgotten.*

Over the years I had experienced many good-byes. I had left this place and that, sometimes for better, sometimes for worse. I felt humble, and my heart was full of hope. My childhood was behind me, and soon I would begin my new life in America. I had wished all my life for this moment.

By the time I arrived at the airport, every muscle in my body was shaking with excitement. I couldn't even hold my hand still to fill out the information sheet. Soon my flight was called. With ticket in hand, I squared my shoulders, boarded the plane, and didn't look back. I felt as though I were walking on air.

I found my seat next to a window. As the engines roared and the plane sped along the runway and took off, I was reminded of my childhood dragon dreams. I watched out the window as the plane started to climb, and I said good-bye to Taiwan. I was glad to be leaving, but still a knot tightened inside me. I blinked away a tear.

As we climbed higher, I spotted a river winding like a blue ribbon till it reached the sea. A voice from my past spoke deep within my heart. I closed my eyes and listened to Favorite Uncle's voice. "The river grows deeper and wider as it flows home to the sea. Like you, Chi Fa. You will grow deeper and wider as you go, and someday you will be home."

Was America the home I had wished for all my life? I did not know, but, fortunately, I finally had the opportunity to find out.

Soon the sky outside the window was milky with dragon clouds. Big dragons, and little ones too, raced by the window until we climbed even higher, and the sky was bright blue again.

It was a long plane ride to America—many, many hours. I stared out the window until nighttime turned the sky black. From a sliver of moon hung one bright star. I thought of Auntie and the wish that I had made on her porch so many years before. "Wishes do come true, Auntie," I whispered.

No other stars twinkled in the sky, but I did not make a wish on the Orphan Star. My thinking was this: *I am on my way to America—I have no reason to wish for more.*

PART VI

AMERICA

1969–Present

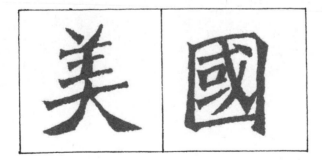

陆启发先生：

您一九＿＿＿年＿＿＿月＿＿＿日来仪要求协助寻访国内亲属事，经国内有关下门邦助查找，已得知您亲属的地址如下：

陆秀珍　上海市车站支路 141弄 58号

中华人民共和国驻美国大使馆领事下

吕平

一九七九年七月四日

The Embassy of the People's Republic of China
helped Lu Chi Fa find his sister.

Epilogue
Two Days
with Sister

(Be Fulfilled)

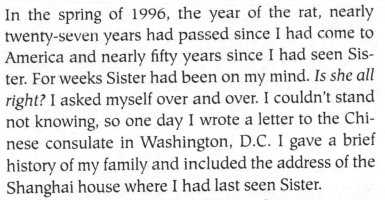

In the spring of 1996, the year of the rat, nearly twenty-seven years had passed since I had come to America and nearly fifty years since I had seen Sister. For weeks Sister had been on my mind. *Is she all right?* I asked myself over and over. I couldn't stand not knowing, so one day I wrote a letter to the Chinese consulate in Washington, D.C. I gave a brief history of my family and included the address of the Shanghai house where I had last seen Sister.

Three weeks passed, and then a letter came stating that the consulate had located my sister. Shiow Jen and Chi Haw still lived on the same street, just a few blocks from the house where I had last seen her. Included in the letter was Sister's new address.

Promptly I wrote her a letter and sent photographs. Within a month, Sister replied with news of her life.

Making the connection with Sister was extraordinary, but more than anything, I wanted to see her again. I decided to go to China. When all the arrangements had been made, I wrote to Sister telling her of my scheduled trip.

By summer's end, I was in Shanghai. I took a taxi from the airport to a modest hotel located about three miles from Sister's house. For me it was the end of a very long day, but in China a new day was dawning. I had taken several long naps on the plane, and now I was too excited to sleep. After checking into my room, I sent a messenger from the hotel to tell Sister I had arrived and would come shortly to see her. I showered, shaved, and put on clean clothes. I gathered the small presents I had brought for her and took a taxi to Sister's.

I was an American citizen, but still I couldn't help feeling a flicker of fear about being in Communist China. I asked the taxi driver to wait. Knocking on the door of Sister's small house, a great sob leaped from my chest. I waited. No one opened the door. My trembling hand knocked again. This time I heard someone open a second-story window. I stepped back and looked up and smiled. It was Chi Haw. I waved. Without even a nod, he slammed the window down and pulled the curtain shut. *Well*, I thought, *some things never change*.

When a third knock, much louder than the first two, brought no one to the door, I thought perhaps

Sister was in the backyard. I walked around to the back of the house. One look, and I knew that Sister must live here. The backyard was crowded with rows of crisp, green vegetable leaves. Peach trees of varied sizes bordered the tiny yard like soldiers guarding the garden. Perhaps, resigned to the fact that she would never leave mainland China, Sister had replanted a peach tree for each daughter and then planted one as each grandchild had come along. The trees' branches hung heavy with plump, ripe, pink-and-yellow fruit. I reached to touch one.

"Help yourself," said a voice behind me. I turned and saw two strangers. "You must be Chi Fa from America," said the man, scurrying over to shake my hand. "My wife and I live in this house with your sister and Chi Haw."

I nodded to his wife. "Where is Sister?" I asked the man.

"You missed Shiow Jen. Upon receiving your message, she hurried off to your hotel to meet you. You probably passed her on your way here."

"Oh dear," I told him, "Sister misunderstood my message."

"Don't worry. She is walking to the hotel. If you take the taxi that's waiting in front, you may get there before she does," said the woman.

I thanked the couple and went back to the road, where the taxi was waiting. "Please take me back to the hotel," I told the driver.

When I reached the hotel, I rushed into the lobby. There she was—beautiful Shiow Jen! Short bobbed hair framed a sweet face. She wore the Communist uniform. I went to her and hugged her hard. We wept. The only sound was our sobs. I didn't ever want to let go of her again. I tried to compose myself, but all I could say was, "Sister."

She seemed surprised. She could not believe that I really was Chi Fa "all grown up." Wiping away tears, I asked, "Were you expecting a little boy?"

Sister laughed, and we hugged again.

For privacy, I ushered her upstairs to my room. I ordered jasmine tea, chilled Chinese pears, and sweets. Although the hotel was modest and would not be considered at all luxurious by American standards, Sister was awed by what she saw as great elegance. We spent the whole day drinking pots of tea and remembering yesterdays. Then we told each other about things that had happened to us since we'd said good-bye in the darkness, on the floor, in Shanghai. When we were both weary from talking and laughing, I invited her to have supper with me at a nearby restaurant.

Stepping carefully, Sister hurried down the stairs and through the lobby, then glided along the street beside me. "Chi Fa, Daughter Number Two says the rice is not good where we are going." Then she stopped and turned to face me. Wagging a finger, she said, "Don't order the fish, either. Number One Son-in-Law says it is never fresh." Hurrying along again, she added, "I have heard that the noodle soup is fairly good, but a little bit too salty and too expensive."

Despite her apprehensions, supper was delicious. Too soon night came like a thief to steal the day from us. After a long hug on the street, I put Sister into a taxi and sent her home. It had been one of the most extraordinary days of my life—one that I would never forget. That night, curled up in bed, I slipped into a peaceful slumber.

The next day, family members who lived in Shanghai gathered on the grass at a nearby park for a picnic. I saw Sister's daughters and their husbands and children. My eldest niece said she remembered when we were children and we had watched the stars together. "When I see bright stars, I always think of you, Uncle Chi Fa," she said.

I saw uncles and aunts—many very ancient now. I saw cousins and met grandnieces and grandnephews, all born after I had left Shanghai. Sister's husband seemed especially proud of his grandsons. We ate delicious Chinese dishes, including salty, double-yolked duck eggs and ripe peaches. My two days in China were good and happy ones.

After the picnic, Sister and I sat alone in her kitchen, sipping tea. In the end, I decided that all was well with her. I could go back to my home in America with a peace-filled heart.

Saying good-bye to Sister was one of the hardest things I had ever done—but I had to. My life was in America. I was flying home early the next morning. As I turned to go, Sister followed me out to the road and hugged me in a long good-bye. "Sister," I told her, "I could not have survived without you."

Sister squeezed my hand. Before my fingers slipped from her grasp, she whispered, "You are lucky, Chi Fa. Good fortune has found you." And as a nearby pair of crickets sang, "All's well. All's well," Sister hurried back inside.

I lingered on the street until her kitchen light winked out and darkness descended like a final curtain. I walked back to the hotel, wondering if I would ever see Sister again, but it was not to be. She died in the spring of 1997, the year of the ox.

Today I own a successful restaurant in California. Over the years, I have found America to be everything that I had heard as a child and much more. I eat three times a day, and, indeed, I am too full to swallow sorrow. My house has many rooms with a view of the Pacific Ocean. Still, to this day, my greatest pleasure is watching the sky. At day's end, when the big red sun sinks into the sea, I think of Papa and Mama, who disappeared early from my life. I know they are not gone forever but will reappear in the dawn of another time.

The sight of dragon-shaped clouds always reminds me of Grandma, who taught me that I was worthwhile. And when the Orphan Star rises, I think of the old man on the island and Auntie—they taught me how to wish for a better life.

Later, when the sky is lit with many stars, I am reminded of Sister, Favorite Uncle, Nephew, and the women who worked in the kitchen on the island— all those who brightened my dark childhood days with love and caring.

Like the stars in the sky, some of those in my past shed a lesser light. They were there to teach me patience and courage; they made me strong. Looking back on my life, I am glad for every person I have known.

I am thankful each night when I curl up in my big soft bed, and if I cannot sleep, I recite Confucius for comfort:

> With coarse rice to eat,
> with water to drink,
> and my bended arm for a pillow—
> I have still joy in the midst of these things.

As I drift off to peaceful sleep, from somewhere in the darkness comes Grandma's voice. "All the way from heaven, your mother reaches long arms and wraps you in love," Grandma whispers. "Very good."

Time Line

1937–1945
The Sino-Japanese War
For most of the war
the Japanese occupy
the major coastal cities.

February 8, 1940
The year of the dragon
begins.

January 27, 1941
The year of the snake
begins.

December, 13, 1941
Lu Chi Fa is born in
Kangsu Province
China.

December 11, 1941
The U.S. declares war
on Japan. China and
the U.S. become allies
in World War II.

February 15, 1942
The year of the horse
begins.

February 5, 1943
The year of the sheep
begins

1943
The U.S. repeals the
Chinese Exclusion
Acts, loosening
restrictions on
emigration from China.

January 25, 1944
The year of the monkey
begins.

Summer 1944
Lu Chi Fa's parents die.

February 13, 1945
The year of the rooster
begins.

All of 1945
Lu Chi Fa is passed
between relatives.

September 2, 1945
Japan surrenders. World
War II ends. China
remains in turmoil:
flooding and starvation
are widespread.

February 2, 1946 The year of the dog begins.	Autumn 1946 Lu Chi Fa is sold to Communist Parents.	*1945–1949* *Chinese Civil War*
January 22, 1947 The year of the pig begins.		
February 10, 1948 The year of the rat begins.	Autumn 1948 Sister rescues Lu Chi Fa. Lu Chi Fa moves in with Favorite Uncle.	
January 29, 1949 The year of the ox begins.	Summer 1949 Lu Chi Fa lives with Grandma. Autumn 1949 Lu Chi Fa moves in with epileptic friend.	October 1, 1949 Nationalists retreat to Taiwan and the People's Republic of China established under Chairman Mao Zedong.
February 17, 1950 The year of the tiger begins.	Spring 1950 Lu Chi Fa moves to Shanghai.	June 28, 1950 Agrarian Reform Laws enacted. Wealthy landowners such as Chi Haw loose land.
February 6, 1951 The year of the rabbit begins.	Autumn 1951 Lu Chi Fa escapes to Hong Kong.	1951 The UN declares sanctions against the People's Republic of China for its role in the Korean War, isolating it politically.
January 27, 1952 The year of the dragon begins.		
February 14, 1953 The year of the snake begins.		
February 3, 1954 The year of the horse begins.	Summer 1954 Lu Chi Fa moves to Taiwan.	

January 24, 1955
The year of the sheep
begins.

Autumn 1955
Lu Chi Fa moves out of
Older Brother's house.

February 12, 1956
The year of the
monkey begins.

January 31, 1957
The year of the rooster
begins.

February 18, 1958
The year of the dog
begins.

1959–1960
In a widespread famine
30 million starve in
mainland China.

February 8, 1959
The year of the pig begins.

January 28, 1960
The year of the rat
begins.

February 15, 1961
The year of the ox begins.

December 1961
Lu Chi Fa is drafted into
the military.

February 5, 1962
The year of the tiger
begins.

January 25, 1963
The year of the rabbit
begins.

December 1963
Lu Chi Fa is discharged
from the military.

February 13, 1964
The year of the dragon
begins.

February 2, 1965
The year of the snake
begins.

January 21, 1966
The year of the horse
begins.

1966
Chairman Mao launches
Cultural Revolution.
Violence and political
chaos ensue.

February 9, 1967
The year of the sheep
begins.

January 30, 1968
The year of the monkey
begins.

February 17, 1969
The year of the
rooster begins.

October 29, 1969
Lu Chi Fa emigrates
to U.S.

February 1972
President Richard M.
Nixon visits the
People's Republic of
China, opening U.S.-
Chinese relations.

September 9, 1976
Chairman Mao dies.

June 4, 1989
Pro-democracy
demonstrations in
Tiananmen Square,
Beijing, end in
violence and a
clampdown on
political dissidents.

February 19, 1996
The year of the rat
begins.

August 1996
Lu Chi Fa visits Sister in
Shanghai, China.